# A MILITARY REVO

## Military Change and Europea

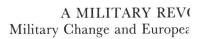

# Studies in European History

General Editor: Richard Overy
Editorial Consultants: John Breuilly
                        Roy Porter

PUBLISHED TITLES

FORTHCOMING

# A MILITARY REVOLUTION?

## Military Change and European Society
## 1550–1800

JEREMY BLACK

MACMILLAN

First published 1991

Published by
MACMILLAN EDUCATION LTD
Houndmills, Basingstoke, Hampshire RG21 2XS
and London
Companies and representatives
throughout the world

Typeset by
Footnote Graphics, Warminster, Wiltshire

Printed in Hong Kong

British Library Cataloguing in Publication Data
Black, Jeremy
A military revolution? : military change and European
society 1550–1800. — (Studies in European history).
1. Military forces. Social aspects, history
I. Title   II. Series
306.27094

ISBN 0–333–51906–X

# Contents

To David and David,
Friends and Fellow-Writers

# Editor's Preface

The main purpose of this new series of studies is to make available to teacher and student alike developments in a field of history that has become increasingly specialised with the sheer volume of new research and literature now produced. These studies are designed to present the 'state of the debate' on important themes and episodes in European history since the sixteenth century, presented in a clear and critical way by someone who is closely concerned himself with the debate in question.

The studies are not intended to be read as extended bibliographical essays, though each will contain a detailed guide to further reading which will lead students and the general reader quickly to key publications. Each book carries its own interpretation and conclusions, while locating the discussion firmly in the centre of the current issues as historians see them. It is intended that the series will introduce students to historical approaches which are in some cases very new and which, in the normal course of things, would take many years to filter down into the textbooks and school histories. I hope it will demonstrate some of the excitement historians, like scientists, feel as they work away in the vanguard of their subject.

The format of the series conforms closely with that of the companion volumes of studies in economic and social history which has already established a major reputation since its inception in 1968. Both series have an important contribution to make in publicising what it is that historians are doing and in making history more open and accessible. It is vital for history to communicate if it is to survive.

R. J. OVERY

# A Note on References

References are cited throughout in square brackets according to the numbering in the Bibliography, with page references where necessary indicated by a colon after the bibliography number.

# Acknowledgements

The illustrations of military weapons and soldiers are reproduced by permission of 'The Mansell Collection'.

# Preface

The importance of the relationship between war and society is well established, but too often the nature of this relationship is obscure and the social dimension has been studied at the expense of military activity. This is particularly dangerous on the European scale when the problem of analysing many armies and lands over many decades can lead to a tendency to generalise on the basis of a few well-studied countries or campaigns. A misleading impression can be created of what is typical and what distinct, and unfounded causal relationships can be advanced.

This brief study seeks to re-examine the so-called Military Revolution of 1560–1660 in order to provide a different account of early modern European military developments. By stressing the relative importance of change after 1660, a different chronology is suggested and it is argued that military change arose from the absolutist state rather than causing it. An alternative basis of absolutism and thus of this change is found in the relative return of domestic stability, specifically acceptable crown-elite relationships, that followed the religious consolidation of several states, particularly France and Austria, in the first half of the seventeenth century. Increases in armed forces encouraged other rulers who wished to play a major role in what was an aggressive competitive international system to follow suit. Any model is of only limited value in face of the European diversity of the period, but it is hoped that the ideas of this work will encourage fresh thought about a number of tired stereotypes.

I am grateful to David Aldridge, Matthew Anderson, David Parrott, Andrew Pettegree, John Plowright, John Stoye and Philip Woodfine for commenting on earlier drafts of this book. The general editor, Richard Overy, has been extremely helpful and I have also benefited from suggestions made by his two colleagues. I would like to thank Michael Prestwich for discussing medieval warfare with me and David Parrott for discussing the Thirty Years War and the French army of the seventeenth century. Gitte and Wendy have coped with my handwriting wonderfully.

JEREMY BLACK

Their expences are almost all employed in rendering themselves terrible to their neighbours; and fortified towns and citadels are the sovereign game they hunt after. Applications of this hostile turn in some, soon make them necessary in all; and we now see the fate of Europe overspread with military grandeur ... it becomes absolutely necessary for every state that would preserve its present existence, to support a considerable body of disciplined troops; and the more so, since the only imaginable resource and security of the weaker, by forming defensive alliances and confederacies, appears in this day to be of no effect. The most solemn engagements are impiously violated.

(Corbyn Morris, *A Letter from a By-Stander to a Member of Parliament: Wherein is Examined What Necessity there is for the Maintenance of a Large Regular Land-Force in this Island* (London, 1742) pp. 6–7. Discussing the rulers of Europe. He refers at the end to the recent attack on Maria Theresa by many of the guarantors of the Habsburg inheritance, especially Frederick the Great of Prussia and Louis XV of France.)

# List of Illustrations

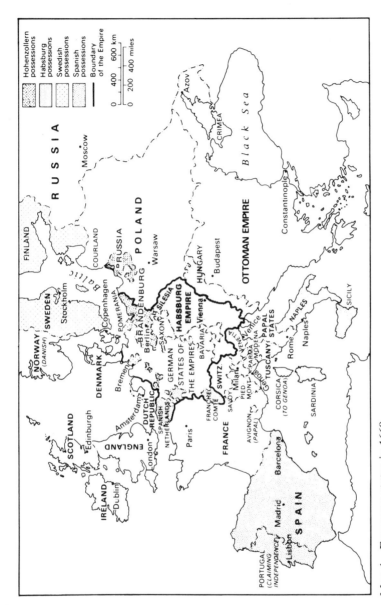

Map 1   European states in 1660

# 1 Military Change

## (i) The theory of the military revolution

*The Roberts' thesis*

The idea that a military revolution occurred in the early modern period, specifically the century 1560–1660, is an established part of the curriculum for early modern studies in Britain. It is based on a published lecture by Michael Roberts, delivered in 1955 and published the following year. This drew essentially on his detailed studies of early-seventeenth-century Sweden, and in particular on the reign of Gustavus Adolphus (1611–32) and on Sweden's entry in 1630 into the Thirty Years War (1618–48) in which most of the Holy Roman Empire (essentially modern Germany and Austria) was involved [1]. The idea is linked commonly with the view that developments in the following century (1660–1760) were of considerably less importance and that the pace of military change resumed in the closing revolutionary decades of the eighteenth century, especially with the outbreak of the French Revolutionary Wars in 1792. The thesis is therefore related to the generally dominant view of early modern European history, one that sees a resolution of earlier crises culminating in a supposed mid-seventeenth-century crisis, followed, after 1660, by relative stability within states and limited wars between them until the onset of an Age of Revolutions. Indeed the putative military revolution has been used to explain this period of stability which is described as the age of absolutism and defined in terms of the authority and power of centralising personal monarchies.

The essentials of the Roberts' thesis are a mutually sustaining relationship between the professionalism required for

1

tactical changes and the rise of larger and more permanent state military forces. Roberts stated that changes in tactics, strategy, the scale of warfare and its impact upon society which had their origins in the United Provinces (modern Netherlands) at the end of the sixteenth century and culminated in the Sweden of Gustavus Adolphus deserved the description 'revolutionary'. Geoffrey Parker summarised the Roberts' thesis as follows:

> First came a 'revolution in tactics': the replacement of the lance and pike by the arrow and musket, as the feudal knights fell before the firepower of massed archers or gunners. Associated with this development were a marked growth in army size right across Europe (with the armed forces of several states increasing tenfold between 1500 and 1700), and the adoption of more ambitious and complex strategies designed to bring these larger armies into action. Fourth and finally, Roberts' military revolution dramatically accentuated the impact of war on society: the greater costs incurred, the greater damage inflicted, and the greater administrative challenge posed by the augmented armies made waging war far more of a burden and far more of a problem than ever previously, both for the civilian population and for their rulers. [4:1–2]

The net result was the creation in the short term of a Swedish army that brought Gustavus Adolphus striking military success, reversing the triumphant run of victories in the early stages of the Thirty Years War by the forces of the Austrian Habsburg Ferdinand II and his allies in the Catholic League [26], and in the long term the creation of armies that were an effective force of statecraft, domestically and externally. These are held to have facilitated the development of absolutist states by shifting the balance of domestic military power towards sovereigns and away from their subjects.

Tactical changes pioneered in the Dutch army were crucial to Roberts' theory of a military revolution. The rise in infantry firepower in the sixteenth century led Count Maurice of Nassau (1567–1625), who assumed the military leadership of the revolt of the Netherlands against Spain after the assassina-

2

tion of his father William of Orange in 1584, to introduce shallower troop formations that permitted more soldiers to fire at once. In the 1590s Maurice and his cousin Count William Louis of Nassau worked out how to put into practice William's idea of maintaining continuous fire by using a volley technique. William had been impressed by Aelian's account of the drill employed by the Roman javelin and sling-shot throwers and he argued that six rotating ranks of musketeers could maintain constant fire. To maximise the effect of this tactical innovation, and increase an army's firepower, a broader battle formation was required. The counts of Nassau retrained the Dutch army in the 1590s so that they became adept in the new tactics, a process that was helped in 1599 when the Dutch States General agreed to provide funds to equip their entire field army with weapons of the same size and calibre [2].

At first ten ranks were needed to maintain constant fire, but Gustavus Adolphus, who was greatly influenced by the Nassau tactical reforms, was able through constant drill and practice to improve Swedish reloading speeds so that by the 1620s only six ranks were needed to maintain continuous fire.

Gustavus followed Maurice in having his troops fight in line but he also stressed the importance of attack. Whereas the Dutch had used the countermarch defensively (the manoeuvre by which musketeers rotated their position by moving through the ranks of their colleagues, so that, having fired, they could retire to reload while others fired), in order to maintain a strong position, Gustavus employed it offensively, the other ranks moving forward through stationary reloaders. He also trained his cavalry to charge in order to break the opposing formation by the impact of the charge and by the use of swords, rather than to approach and fire guns from horseback. The effectiveness of the Swedish army was demonstrated at the battle of Breitenfeld in 1631, when the imperial army under Tilly, which had hitherto been a successful force, was defeated by Gustavus' Swedish troops after their Saxon allies had broken.

Firing by rank required both discipline and training and this led to an increase in the number of officers and the produc-tion of detailed training manuals. More complex manoeuvres

3

required more training and discipline and this could best be ensured by maintaining permanent forces, rather than hastily hiring men at the outbreak of wars. The new armies turned infantry firepower into a manoeuvrable winning formula, allowing rulers to envisage victorious campaigns. This enhanced the value of larger armies rather than fortifications but these more substantial forces required a level of administrative support, in the supply of money, men and provisions, that led to new governmental institutions and larger financial demands. The domestic strains thus created helped to cause a mid-seventeenth-century crisis in much of Europe [106, 127], but the Roberts' model holds that armies enhanced monarchical power sufficiently to ensure that in most states an effective royal monopoly of power was created. This monopolisation furthered and was then in turn furthered by a militarisation of society, that owed much to military service, including the growth of noble officership and of conscription, and to the centrality of military needs in administration. Military requirements and their ethos integrated society and the state. Thus, the modern art of war, with its large professional armies and concentrated yet mobile firepower, was created at the same time as – indeed, made possible and necessary – the creation of the modern state.

### The Parker variation

Roberts' thesis has been generally accepted. Since its publication the principal contribution to the debate has come from Geoffrey Parker's work on Spain, though this has essentially modified the details of the thesis rather than revising it substantially. Parker used his detailed knowledge of the leading army in western Europe, that of the Habsburg kings of Spain [21], a force regarded as conservative by Roberts, to suggest that he was wrong to see only the Dutch and Swedes as progressive. Arguing that the Spaniards were in fact flexible in infantry and cavalry tactics and training [3], Parker proposed that the period of transformation, 1560–1660, should be extended back into fifteenth-century Europe when the impetus was the need to face changes in fortifications resulting from the introduction of gunpowder. Cannon balls could bring down tall, thin walls, English towns in Normandy and Gascony falling to Charles VII in 1450–3, while his grandson Charles VIII enjoyed similar, though more short-lived, success in the Italian wars, which began with his invasion of Italy in 1494. In response, bastions, generally quadrilateral, angled and at regular intervals along all walls, were introduced to provide effective flanking fire while defences were lowered and strengthened with earth. Stronger defences obliged attacking forces to resort to sieges with extensive lines of blockade and thus to employ larger numbers. Stressing the importance of new fortification methods, the *trace italienne*, Parker directs attention away from Gustavus Adolphus:

> the improvements in artillery in the fifteenth century, both qualitative and quantitative, eventually transformed fortress design ... the increasing reliance on firepower in battle – whether with archers, field artillery or musketeers – led not only to the eclipse of cavalry by infantry in most armies, but to new tactical arrangements that maximized the opportunities of giving fire ... these new ways in warfare were accompanied by a dramatic increase in army size ... all the evidence for radical military change, whether in army size, fortifications, or firearms comes from the lands of the Habsburgs or of their neighbours: from Spain, Italy, the Netherlands, and France. That was the heartland of the military revolution.

In a footnote Parker paradoxically excludes 'most of Spain' from the military revolution for the same reason that he asserts that it was limited outside the heartland:

> The key variable appears to have been the presence or absence of the *trace italienne* for where no bastions existed, wars of manoeuvre with smaller armies were still feasible. And, for a long time, outside the 'heartland' there was a marked reluctance to introduce the new defensive systems. [4:24, 26]

Though Parker has clarified his view of when the military revolution began, he is unclear when it ended and his

5

treatment of the post-1660 period is cursory. However, he has argued not only as Roberts did, that the military changes played a crucial role in both states and societies, but also that they were instrumental in shifting the world military balance of power towards Europe, with major consequences in many fields.

Nevertheless, Parker notes that the leading Asiatic powers were not defeated until the nineteenth century, in large part because of their independent military developments, which were especially impressive in Japan where bastioned fortifications were constructed and where a system of volley-fire was being practised as early as the 1560s [4].

Thus, the military changes of the period are seen as having far more than simply military consequences and they can be and have been used to explain developments in a number of fields. However, leaving aside the problem of whether the concept of a revolution lasting a century or longer is really helpful [5], it is far from clear that any military revolution ocurred in the early modern period. It is also possible to claim that the major changes that did occur were concentrated in the century after that customarily associated with the revolution. This is certainly true with regard to the size of the armies of a number of the leading powers, Austria, Britain, France, Prussia and Russia. These have been variously assessed.

European army sizes, 1470–1760

| Date (circa) | Spanish monarchy | Dutch Republic | France | England | Sweden | Russia |
|---|---|---|---|---|---|---|
| 1475 | 20,000 | – | 40,000 | 25,000 | – | – |
| 1555 | 150,000 | – | 50,000 | 10,000 | – | – |
| 1595 | 200,000 | 20,000 | 80,000 | 30,000 | 15,000 | – |
| 1635 | 300,000 | 50,000 | 150,000 | – | 45,000 | 35,000 |
| 1655 | 100,000 | – | 100,000 | 70,000 | 70,000 | – |
| 1675 | 70,000 | 110,000 | 120,000 | 15,000 | 63,000 | 130,000 |
| 1705 | 50,000 | 100,000 | 400,000 | 87,000 | 100,000 | 170,000 |
| 1760 | 98,000 | 36,000 | 247,000 | 199,000 | 85,000 | 146,000 |

Source: G. Parker, 'Warfare', in *New Cambridge Modern History*, XIII, p. 205.

The figures for France in 1635 and 1705 and for Britain in 1760 are too high and that for Russia in 1760 is probably too low. The source of Parker uses for the 1760 figures is unreliable.

European army sizes, 1632–1786

| Date | France | Dutch Republic | Sweden | Russia | Austria | England | Prussia |
|------|--------|----------------|--------|--------|---------|---------|---------|
| 1632 |        | 70,000 | 120,000 | 35,000 |        |        |         |
| 1640 |        |        |        |        |        |        | 4,650   |
| 1653 |        |        |        |        |        |        | 1,800   |
| 1661 | 48,900 |        |        |        |        |        |         |
| 1678 | 280,000 |       |        |        |        |        | 45,000  |
| 1679 | 130,000 |       |        |        |        |        |         |
| 1680 |        |        |        | 200,000 |       |        |         |
| 1688 |        |        |        |        |        | 53,000 | 30,000  |
| 1690 | 338,000 | 73,000 | 90,000 |      | 50,000 | 80,000 |         |
| 1697 |        |        |        |        |        | 90,000 |         |
| 1710 | 360,000 | 100,000 |      | 220,000 | 100,000 |      | 39,000  |
| 1717 | 110,000 |       |        |        |        |        |         |
| 1725 |        |        |        | 215,000 |       |        |         |
| 1738 | 115,000 |       |        |        |        |        |         |
| 1740 | 160,000 |       |        | 240,000 | 108,000 |     | 80,000  |
| 1756 | 330,000 | 39,000 |      | 344,000 | 201,000 |     | 143,000 |
| 1760 |        |        |        |        |        |        | 260,000 |
| 1778 |        |        |        |        | 200,000 | 100,000 | 160,000 |
| 1786 | 156,000 |       |        |        |        |        | 194,000 |

Sources: Several, principally [29, 39].

These figures should be used with care. Any attempt to advance a general pattern must take note of the contrast between figures for war years, such as 1710, and those for peace, such as 1786.

The problems of assessing army size are compounded by the difficulty of deciding which units to include; the nature and military use of garrison and militia units varied. Governments commonly exaggerated the size of their armies, while officers who wished to avoid problems and to embezzle pay overlooked death, disease and desertion in order to present their units as up to strength. Despite these statistical problems, it is clear that there were more men under arms in Europe in the war years of the mid-eighteenth century, 1733–5, 1741–8, 1756–63, than in those of the mid-seventeenth century, and the contrast is even greater if periods of peace across all or most of Europe are considered, for example 1660–4 and 1764–7. As will be shown, it is not only over the issue of the size of armies that the Roberts' thesis is vulnerable.

## (ii) 1560–1660 reassessed

Two principal criticisms can be made of the Roberts' thesis. The first is the extent to which stress on the period 1560–1660 minimises the role of change in earlier centuries; in the second place that the situation in the last decades of the century 1560–1660 scarcely suggests that a revolution was nearly complete. It could also be argued that Roberts devoted too much attention to battlefield tactics and not enough to other aspects of military activity. Such judgements, like the Roberts' thesis itself, must necessarily be regarded as provisional in the absence of a detailed assessment of the military situation throughout Europe, for which much of the necessary work has not yet been undertaken, especially on eastern Europe.

*Warfare before the period of the military revolution*

For several centuries major land encounters had generally involved a mixture of cavalry and infantry, and of firepower and hand-to-hand combat. This remained the case throughout the early modern period and was to continue until mechanised rapid fire reduced the role of hand-to-hand combat and led to the fusion of cavalry and artillery in tank warfare. The nature of these mixtures, especially the weaponry and tactics employed, varied and it is difficult to know on what criteria any variation or number of changes can be regarded as revolutionary. Cases have been made for the revolutionary consequences both of the adoption of the stirrup in the eighth century, which made it possible to use horsemen as shock troops, and of the use of gunpowder in artillery (fourteenth century) and hand-held firearms (fifteenth) towards the end of the Middle Ages [7]. Both developments arguably were more revolutionary in tactical and general social consequences than any changes between 1560 and 1660. In western Europe the importance of cavalry had been challenged by the English use of longbowmen against the French in the thirteenth century and by the Swiss pikemen who had defeated Charles the Bold of Burgundy's cavalry at Grandson and Morat in 1476. The longbow, like the crossbow, was to be replaced as the dominant missile weapon in the early sixteenth century by hand-held firearms, as effective musketry was developed, while the pike was perforce to share its position as principal infantry weapon with them. From the Italian wars of that period until the 1690s infantry warfare involved forces armed with both pikes and firearms. These arms were not fused until the introduction of the socket bayonet and the disappearance of the pike at the end of the seventeenth century, well after the Roberts' period. In contrast, most cavalrymen had long been armed with both guns and swords, their firing and stabbing weapons being lighter than those of the infantry.

In the early sixteenth century the gunpowder firearm used was the arquebus. It was steadily refined by improving the method of firing. Initially a match had to be dabbed against a touch-hole to ignite the powder, but this was replaced first by the matchlock and then, in part from the 1520s, by the wheellock, in which a piece of pyrite was held against a rapidly turning steel wheel, set off by a spring when the trigger was pressed. Thus the nature of firearms was far from constant and the background against which subsequent changes in the so-called early modern period should be judged is one of the infantry weaponry that was already changing considerably. The crossbow largely disappeared from battle in the 1520s. The importance of the arquebus was demonstrated in the defeat of the Swiss pike in French service at Bicocca in 1522 and of the French cavalry at Pavia in 1525, both achieved by mixed Spanish forces remaining on the defensive and relying heavily on firepower. Both were crucial battles in the Italian wars, a series of conflicts fought between 1494 and 1559 in which control of Italy was a major goal and which, from the formation of the anti-French Holy League of 1511, were increasingly characterised by a struggle between France and the Habsburgs. However, as armies developed tactics that did not pitch vulnerable forces against shot, so the edge gained by using it diminished. In comparison to the Italian wars, when there were significant differences between armies in weaponry and tactics, the following period, that of the so-called military revolution, was to be characterised in western Europe by marked similarities in weaponry and tactics [12, 13].

Because of these similarities battles were usually won by experienced and motivated troops whose dispositions had been well arranged. Chance played a considerable role, but the ability of generals and reserves to respond to generally unplanned developments was also important. Gustavus' great victory over the imperial forces at Breitenfeld in 1631 was due in large part to his numerical superiority, always an important if not crucial factor, to the resilience of the Swedish forces in the face of the collapse of their inexperienced Saxon allies, and to the extent to which the Swedish defensive position allowed them to use their firepower against the attacking troops of Tilly's army. Not only did western European forces use the same weapons; they also employed similar tactics. It is a mistake to assume that while the Dutch and Swedes adopted new tactics, other armies stood still and continued to fight in large and relatively undifferentiated formations. The importance of mercenaries and the ready hiring of foreign officers and troops held to ensure a relative universality of tactics, as did the recruitment of prisoners. The Dutch forces trained by Maurice of Nassau were essentially mercenaries as were the vast majority of Gustavus' troops in Germany. About one-sixth of Gustavus' army were Scots. Thus the clearly differentiated forces that might have aided markedly different tactical traditions to develop did not exist, with the important exception of the Turks. Infantry formations generally became less deep, the exact relationship between pike and shot depending in great part on the size and nature of particular units and the lie of the land [23]. Henry IV of France (1594–1610) sought to organise his infantry in units of 500, trained to support each other in line or chequer formation [17].

The battles of the Thirty Years War, unlike some of the famous encounters in the Italian wars, were not generally determined by different tactics and weaponry. Instead their results reflected differing experience and morale and if forces were fairly evenly matched in terms of veterans they were either inconclusive encounters or determined by other factors, such as terrain, the availability and employment of reserves and the results of the cavalry encounters on the flanks which,

Fig. 1   Exercise of the Pike

11

if conclusive, could lead to the victorious cavalry attacking their opponent's infantry in flank or rear, as happened at the Spanish defeat at Rocroi (1643). Duke Bernard of Saxe-Weimar, a German prince who served Sweden in 1630–5 before transferring with the army he had raised to French service, won a number of battles by outmanoeuvring his opponents, outflanking them and attacking them in the rear. At Jankov (1645) the Swedes under Torstensson were initially unable to defeat the Austrian force, which was also about 15,000 strong, but finally won as a result of outmanoeuvring their opponents and attacking them from the rear. The Austrians lost their army, the Swedes benefited from the tactical flexibility of their more experienced force.

Indeed victory commonly went to the larger army and the more experienced force rather than to that which had adopted Dutch-style tactics. At Rocroi there were 24,000 French to 17,000 Spaniards; at the White Mountain (1620) 28,000 in the army of the Catholic League against 21,000 Bohemians and German Protestants; at Nördlingen (1634) 33,000 Catholics to 25,000 Protestants; at Breitenfeld Gustavus Adolphus outnumbered his opponents by 42,000 to 35,000. Breitenfeld was the largest battle, in terms of manpower, of the war and exceptionally so for a conflict in which field armies were rarely more than 30,000 strong and the creation of larger forces posed major logistical problems. Lützen (1632), where the two forces were about the same, each 19,000 strong, was partly for that reason essentially inconclusive.

The Saxons at Breitenfeld adopted the Dutch tactics of small units deployed in relatively narrow formations, but they broke when the Austrians attacked. Ernest, Count of Mansfeld, a leading anti-Habsburg general of the early years of the war, also adopted Dutch tactics without conspicuous success. Victory tended in general to go to larger armies, especially if more experienced, as the Spaniards, Swedes, Weimarians and some of the Austrian and Bavarian units were. Saxe-Weimar rejected the Dutch tactics and in the late 1630s used his heavily cavalry-based army, which was essentially self-sustaining, to fight in an aggressive fashion. Thus, consideration of the battles of the period

12

suggests that Roberts' stress on new infantry tactics is misleading. Campaigns could be conclusive, though this was the case less commonly, and principally when a relatively small state was attacked by a more formidable power, as rebellious Bohemia was in 1620 and Denmark was by imperial forces in 1626–9 and by the Swedes in 1643–5, 1658 and 1700. By the Peace of Lübeck of 1629 the defeated Christian IV of Denmark was obliged to promise never again to interfere in the internal affairs of the Empire. In general, however, campaigns were inconclusive, suggesting that the 'revolution' discerned by Roberts had not solved the basic military problem of securing decisive victory. The inconclusive character of warfare owed much to problems with the supply of men, money and provisions, and to the strength of fortifications [22, 23, 25]. It is particularly apparent in the second, less studied, half of the Thirty Years War, and during the Franco-Spanish and Portuguese-Spanish conflicts of 1635–59 and 1640–68, the last major conflicts in western Europe during the period of Roberts' revolution. Some battles had impressive results. The Austro-Spanish victory at Nördlingen drove the Swedes from southern Germany and led to a settlement of German problems by the Preliminaries of Pirna (1634) and the Peace of Prague (1635) that was accepted by most of the princes of the Empire. In 1638 Bernard of Saxe-Weimar's victory at Rheinfelden over the Austrians and the successful siege of Breisach consolidated French control of Alsace. However, the results of other battles were soon reversed. The Swedish victory over Austro-Saxon troops at Wittstock (1636) was followed by the overrunning of Brandenburg, and the invasion of Saxony, the two leading Protestant allies of Austria, but the following year the Swedes were pushed back to Pomerania by the Austrians and the Saxons. In late 1638 the Swedes, helped by French subsidies, advanced, driving the Austrians into Silesia, while in 1639 they defeated the Saxons near Chemnitz and reached Prague, but were unable to capture it, and were in turn obliged to withdraw from Bohemia. In 1640 the juncture of French and Swedish troops at Erfurt, their first combined operation, had no strategic consequence. In 1645 the French won the second battle of Nördlingen but had to withdraw as

13

they could not maintain their troops, while the Swedes defeated an Austrian army at Jankov and advanced to near Vienna, but then had to retire.

The French triumphs at Rocroi (1643) and Lens (1648) in the Franco-Spanish war were offset by defeats and logistical problems. The consequences of Rocroi have commonly been exaggerated: the Spaniards speedily regrouped. Far from the Spanish empire collapsing, the war ended in a compromise peace, that of the Pyrenees (1659). This was after the intervention of fresh English forces on the side of France had tipped the balance in Flanders, Cromwell's Ironsides helping Turenne to defeat the Spanish army of Flanders at the battle of the Dunes in 1658. The Spanish army was outnumbered, its artillery had not arrived, the terrain prevented it from taking advantage of its superiority in cavalry and its flank was bombarded by English warships. England was rewarded with Dunkirk, which fell after the battle, only to see the recently restored Charles II sell it off to Louis XIV in 1662. French attempts to invade Italy led to repeated failures, as in 1635.

Until rebellious Catalonia was reconquered in 1652 Philip IV devoted few resources to the attempt to reconquer Portugal and the war was essentially a small-scale matter of raids and plundering. Spain launched invasion attempts of Portugal in 1657–9, 1663 and 1665. All were unsuccessful. In 1657–9 Spain, still fighting France with her new English ally, lacked sufficient soldiers. Though various systems for raising troops were employed, the government relied on a contract one, whereby individuals formed units in return for payment. The successive political and military crises of 1635–68 with their rise in Spanish commitments and their heavy losses of men strained the system and, while the cost of raising troops by contract rose rapidly, it became more difficult to field sufficient forces. In 1663 Philip IV, now at peace with all bar Portugal, concentrated his forces, stiffened by all who could be recruited, including criminals, against her, only to face defeat at Ameixial, at the hands of patriotic Portuguese levies supported by a regiment of Cromwell's veterans, sent by Charles II, who had married a Portuguese princess. Two years later defeat at Villaviciosa ended the hope of reconquering Portugal.

14

The most conclusive campaigns of this period occurred in civil wars where it was generally the case that a long conflict was regarded as undesirable and combatants were internally divided and thus, in part, willing to settle. In addition, the geographical scale of conflict was smaller, and the extent of military preparedness less than in conflicts between rulers. Furthermore, modern fortifications were largely concentrated in frontier zones, rather than in the interior of countries. The major fortification projects carried out in Tudor England were at Berwick against the Scots and by Henry VIII on the Channel coast against the possibility of a French invasion. These did not play a significant role in the Civil Wars. The First (1642–6) and Second (1648) Civil Wars were ended by victories by the anti-Royalist forces [15]. Catalonia, which had rebelled against Spain in 1640 [114], was regained, Barcelona falling in 1652. This achievement, on the part of a state commonly presented as in terminal decline, has never received sufficient attention, in contrast to the rebellion.

If the supposed flagship of military change, the Swedish army, could be defeated at Nördlingen (1634) and enjoyed less than complete success at Lützen (1632), the French had a whole series of defeats in the 1630s and 1640s. Major defeats included Fuenterrabia in 1638, when a French besieging army under Condé was defeated by the Spaniards, and the Austrian victory at Thionville the following year. Though the Spanish army of Flanders, which had beaten the French at Honne-court in 1642, was defeated at Rocroi by them in 1643, later the same year the French army in Germany was defeated at Tuttlingen by the Bavarians and forced to retreat to the Rhine, abandoning its baggage and losing most of its men in the winter retreat. The Bavarians defeated the French again at Freiburg (1644) and Mergentheim (1645), only to lose to a French-Swedish army at Allerheim in 1645. French invasions of northern Italy, in 1635–6, 1638 and the mid-1640s, were unsuccessful, their forces being driven back, for example at Vercelli in 1638, and suffering from supply problems and desertion. After 1643 it was less a question of French defeats than of a failure to make much progress, certainly progress commensurate with the need to defeat Spain before French finances collapsed. Dunkirk fell in 1647, but it, and other

French gains, were lost when Spain took advantage of the *Fronde*, the French civil wars of 1648–53. The end of the *Fronde* did not bring victory for France. Defeats at Pavia (1655) and Valenciennes (1656) led France to offer reasonable terms only for Philip IV to reject them in 1656. Valenciennes was a spectacular victory, but the somewhat deterministic notions of the inevitability of the decline of Spain that are widely held ensure that it does not enjoy the fame of Rocroi.

A recent thesis on the French army in this period has revealed the weakness of French military administration, helping to explain why their campaigns were often fruitless. Under Louis XIII and his leading minister Cardinal Richelieu, France went to war with Spain in 1635, hoping to achieve victory in one campaign. Like Philip IV of Spain and his first minister, the Duke of Olivares, they did not seek a lengthy, defensive or attritional war. However, it proved impossible to create the large armies required to achieve the bold strategic conceptions that were devised [24]. The Protestant Duke Henri de Rohan, who had rebelled against Louis XIII in 1626–9, discovered that his troops were no better supplied when he fought for Louis against Spain in 1635–6. In the 1620s his troops had been poorly equipped and disciplined and lacked pay and food. The royal general, the Prince of Condé, employed exactions in the Vivarais in the winter of 1627–8 to persuade the Protestants not to back Rohan and to support his own troops. By 1635 Rohan was in the Valtelline passes between Austria and Spanish-ruled Lombardy, operating in snows waist deep and without sufficient food, fodder or money for his troops. In 1636 he invaded Lombardy but found his officers unwilling to abandon the booty they had gained in the Valtelline, his troops affected by disease and mutinous because of lack of pay. Without cannon and munitions, Rohan dared not move into the Lombard plain. The following year he had to abandon his fortresses in the Valtelline because he had no money.

Such circumstances made coherent planning impractical and joint operations by allies difficult. In 1634–5 Duke Maximilian of Bavaria, the head of the Catholic League, quarrelled with his ally the Emperor Ferdinand II over troop quarters, the disposition of booty and ransoms and the allocation of

16

Spanish subsidies, as well as continuing a long-running clash over priorities with Maximilian seeking a concentration upon south Germany and Ferdinand upon Bohemian operations. Supply difficulties and their consequences in the shape of desertion led generals to campaign in areas whence they could obtain substantial enforced contributions and the protection of these areas from opposing forces became a major feature of military activity. Troops were dispersed to forage and to man positions protecting supply zones and many, mostly small-scale, encounters arose from raids and from attempts to define contribution zones. In these engagements the writings of battlefield theorists were of no value. Far from actions being characterised by linear formations and interspersed shot and pike, they were commonly dominated by considerations of surprise, energy and topography, in which training was less important than morale and leadership. Similar encounters marked most of the sieges of the period. Complete lines of circumvallation designed to cut off the chance of relief required many troops and were generally found only in the case of major sieges. Similarly only a minority of towns were comprehensively fortified in accordance with contemporary ideals of bastions and flanking fire, for such fortifications were extremely expensive. Thus, alongside the set-piece major sieges, such as the successful Spanish siege of Dutch-held Ostend in 1601–4, the Spanish capture of Breda from the Dutch in 1625 and the French taking of Perpignan from Spain in 1642, there were numerous minor engagements, as towns were stormed or relieving parties attacked [10]. The idea of battlefield or siege techniques as causing and in part constituting a military revolution pays insufficient attention to the inchoate nature of much fighting and military organisation in this period. The strains of prolonged warfare led rulers to desire effective military instruments, but they also made them difficult to provide. It is difficult to see how the warfare of the mid-seventeenth century justified the theory of a military revolution.

*Eastern Europe*

This is also the case if attention is devoted to fighting in eastern Europe during the last years of the so-called military revolution. There were important developments in the Polish and Russian armies in the first half of the seventeenth century. Gustavus Adolphus had attacked Poland in 1617–18, 1621–2 and 1625–9, capturing the important Baltic port of Riga in 1621, after a siege in which he used creeping barrages (systematically advancing artillery bombardment), and over-running Livonia in 1625. These campaigns helped to ensure that Gustavus, his officers and men were battle-hardened when he invaded Germany in 1630. Polish defeats, which contrasted with their earlier cavalry victories over the Swedes at Kirchholm (1605) and Klushino (1610), spurred the Poles to consider new ideas, leading in 1632–3 to the creation of musketeer units and an attempt to standardise the artillery, which increased in size. Imitating the Swedes, the Poles introduced three-to-six-pounder regimental guns between 1633 and 1650. The Russian government, conscious of Swedish developments and dissatisfied with the *Streltsy*, the permanent infantry corps equipped with handguns founded in 1550, decided in 1630 to form 'new order' military units, officered mostly by foreigners. Ten such regiments, totalling about 17,000 men, amounted to half the Russian army in the War of Smolensk with Poland (1632–4).

However, it is important not to exaggerate the extent or success of military change in eastern Europe. In 1632–4 the Russian siege of Smolensk, which had been extensively forti-fied by them in 1595–1602 before being lost to Poland as a result of the Time of Troubles (1604–13), the period of internal instability and foreign invasion caused by a disputed succession to the throne, was unsuccessful, the Russians losing all bar 8,000 of their 35,000-man army. In 1634, at the end of the war, the new units were demobilised and foreign mercen-aries were ordered to leave. Despite the improvements to the Polish army, the number of their infantry and dragoons was only a few thousand in 1655 when Charles X of Sweden invaded, seizing Warsaw and Cracow, while their artillery was inadequate. Having been defeated at Zarnow and Wojnicz in 1655, the Poles avoided battle with large Swedish formations from March 1656, preferring to use the element of surprise [19].

Rather than seeing the Poles and Russians as slow developers in some league table of revolutionary European military change, it is worth pointing out that their armed forces had to be able not only to fight 'western' style armies, such as the Swedes, but also to resist the still militarily very powerful Turks and their Tatar allies, who invaded Poland in 1621. This was a fast-moving confrontation involving light cavalry and fortified camps, in which battles were largely cavalry engagements and tactics involving slow-moving linear infantry formations were inappropriate. In contrast, the Austro-Turkish conflict of 1593–1606 was largely a war of sieges in and near the valley of the Danube, suggesting that it would be foolish to contrast eastern and western European warfare too readily. The logistical strength of the Turkish army in this war was impressive. The supply-line through Hungary was helped by the rivers which flow north/south: after Belgrade men, equipment and supplies could be transported along the Danube or the Tisza. An efficient supply system moved food from Hungary and the Danubian principalities to the front. Troops could march the 600 miles from Constantinople to Buda in six weeks at an average daily speed of 15–20 miles, drawing for provisions on forty depots. In the conflict-zone the troops were supplied from magazines set up by the army establishment. The soliders were well fed, receiving meat regularly, and the pay was not generally in arrears, in marked contrast with the situation in most of Europe. The 'Ottoman road' from Constantinople to Buda and beyond helped ensure a level of efficiency in Turkish military administration that was greater than that elsewhere [64], though it would be misleading to suggest that Turkish campaigns on other fronts were always characterised by such efficiency and ease of operation.

It would be inaccurate to suggest that 'new style' tactics were necessarily successful against the Poles and the Russians. Just as the Dutch did not sweep to victory over Spain after the adoption of the Nassau reforms, so Gustavus was unable to defeat the Polish general Koniecpolski in his Prussian campaigns of 1626–9. Concerned about the strength of the Polish cavalry, Gustavus was unwilling to meet the Poles in the open without the protection of fieldworks, while Polish cavalry attacks on supply lines and small units impeded Swedish operations. Czarniecki used similar tactics of harassment successfully in 1656, obliging the Swedes, who could not maintain their supplies, to withdraw. The Russo-Polish conflict in 1654–67 was characterised by mobile warfare in which light cavalry units played an important role. The techniques of countermarching and volley fire were not without relevance in eastern Europe, but the small number of engagements fought between linear formations of infantry and settled by firepower is a reminder that these tactical innovations were not the only ones of importance. On the evidence of Eastern Europe they can hardly be seen as the key to a European military revolution.

## (iii) Change 1660–1760

In so far as decisive developments occurred during the period 1560–1760, in the case of most military forces they were primarily found in the second half of the period. This was certainly true of Austria, Britain, France, Prussia and Russia. It was also true of naval warfare in general and of second-rank powers including, in particular, Savoy-Piedmont [136]. It was arguably the failure of Poland and Turkey to witness similar changes that played a major role in their international difficulties in the eighteenth century.

*Weaponry and tactics*

In weaponry and tactics the principal innovation was the disappearance of the pike and the consequent arming of all infantrymen with the same weapon, a musket fitted with a bayonet. This increased firepower and both the offensive and defensive capacity of the infantry. The change was a rapid one and largely carried out in the 1690s and early 1700s. Brandenburg-Prussia adopted the bayonet in 1689, Denmark in 1690. The French abandoned the pike in 1703, the British in 1704. At the battle of Fleurus (1690) some German units attracted attention by repulsing French cavalry attacks although armed only with muskets and unsupported by pikes.

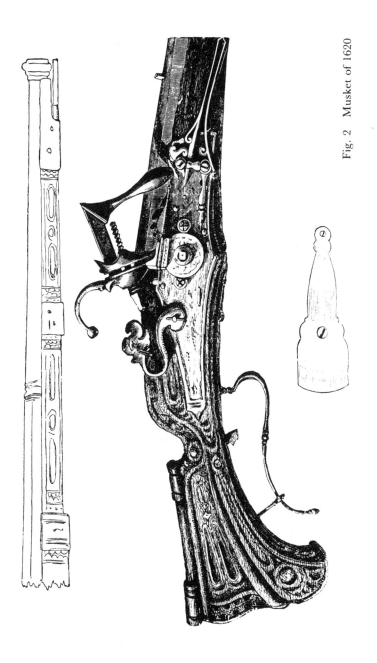

Fig. 2  Musket of 1620

At the same time the matchlock was replaced by the lighter, less unreliable and more rapid-firing flintlock musket, whose powder was ignited by a spark produced through the action of flint on steel. The new guns were lighter, not requiring a rest, and easier to fire, while the rate of fire, helped by the spread of paper cartridges, almost doubled. The flintlock was the standard weapon in the Dutch, English and French armies by 1700, the Austrians adopted it between the 1680s and the 1700s and the Swedes introduced it in 1696. The flintlock was made more effective by the replacement in this period of the early plug bayonets, which hindered firing, by ring and socket bayonets, which allowed firing with the blade in place.

Whereas it was very complicated to coordinate pikemen and musketeers in order to ensure the necessary balance of defensive protection and firepower, the use of bayonets ensured that the tactical flexibility of infantry increased substantially. Maximum firepower was ensured by linear formations and shoulder-to-shoulder drill, but lines became longer and thinner than earlier in the century. Casualty rates rose appreciably and in most eighteenth-century battles injuries were caused by gunshot and not by hand-to-hand combat. The combination of the adoption of these changes by all powers, with the exception of the Turks and the Poles, and of higher casualty rates did not prevent decisive battles. One of the armies that changed the most was the Austrian. Count Raimondo Montecuccoli (1609–80), an Italian who had been captured by the Swedes at Breitenfeld in 1631 and again in 1639, and who rose to be Commander-in-Chief and President of the War Council 1668–80, made the army more mobile by reducing the size of units. He also cut the number of men armed with pikes, increased the number of musketeers, copied the Swedish use of light field artillery and reduced the amount of the cavalry's armour in order to increase their mobility. After his death pikes were replaced by bayonets in the Austrian army [32]. Austrian success against the Turks in 1683–99 and 1716–18, not least the ability to wage successive offensive campaigns, owed much to Montecuccoli's reforms.

Another army that changed considerably was that of France. A growing awareness of the limitations of Richelieu's achievements necessarily throws those of Louis XIV into prominence. During his reign the administration of the rapidly increasing army was improved. In essence the king and his ministers sought, with a measure of success, to gain control over the army. The payment of troops was regulated; drill, training and equipment were considerably standardised and distinctive uniforms were introduced. The name of the Inspector-General of the Infantry and commander of the *Régiment du Roi*, Martinet, entered the language as the description of a strict disciplinarian. The command structure was revised, a contentious matter in a society where social hierarchy could conflict with military seniority. It was only under Louis XIV that a major programme of new fortifications was pursued: under Louis XIII there had been major works, for example at Pinerolo, but nothing that compared with the systematic attempt to defend vulnerable frontier regions with new fortifications that his son supported. The supply system, of men, money, munitions and provisions, was considerably improved, and a system of *étapes* (depots), was created to support it. These achievements owed much to two successive Secretaries for War, Michel Le Tellier and his son Louvois. This new and daunting military force was applied with considerable effect under the inspired leadership of Condé, Turenne and Luxembourg. Luxembourg, who employed independently operating advance units, was one of the originators of the divisional system. However, the French army was not invariably successful. Louis XIV's failure to secure the limited and short wars he sought in 1672 and 1688 tested the strength of his army, as it was obliged to confront major European coalitions, while the French generals of the War of the Spanish Succession (1701–14), though not without talent, as Villars demonstrated [61], were in several cases outmanoeuvred by the Duke of Marlborough and Prince Eugene, the leading British and Austrian generals [37]. The greater ministerial control that had been achieved in the 1660s was not sustained in full during the major wars that began in 1672. Furthermore, the Nine Years (1688–97) and Spanish Succession wars placed major strains on the system of army supplies. Much of the fighting was on or near French territory which became exhausted as the conflicts lasted for many years, and economic circumstances were generally harsh.

Fig. 3  Pikeman *circa* James I

Fig. 4    Musketeer *circa* James I

There were years of poor harvests and higher than normal mortality rates, which affected the supply of food and men. In 1709–10, a period of especially harsh economic conditions, the system of supplying the army through negotiating contracts with army suppliers broke down, as the government could no longer afford it, and it was instead obliged to attempt an experiment with providing supplies through government officials, the *intendants* and the *commissaires de guerre*.

*Decisive battles*

It is easy to point to indecisive engagements or to those in which neither army was badly defeated, for example, among the battles in the Low Countries during the Nine Years War, Steenkerk (1692). There were others that were important in their consequences. The Prussian victory over the Swedes at Fehrbellin (1675) ended the Swedish hope of making gains at the expense of Brandenburg-Prussia and signalled militarily a shift in the balance of power in north Germany from Sweden to Prussia. William III's victory at the Boyne in 1690, at the head of an army of British, Dutch and Danish troops, over James II, at the head of a Franco-Irish force, settled the fate of Ireland. The Jacobite army on the southern bank of the river Boyne was defeated on both flanks. The following year at Aughrim the Jacobite flank was turned when cavalry of the Anglo-Dutch army crossed a bog on which hurdles had been laid. Tactical flexibility was crucial in these Irish battles. Peter the Great's defeat of Charles XII at Poltava in 1709 was another decisive battle. It led to the collapse of Swedish hopes to exploit Ukrainian disaffection in order to weaken Russia fatally and was followed by the overrunning of Sweden's eastern Baltic provinces [52].

In the War of the Spanish Succession the Anglo-Dutch-Austrian victory at Blenheim (1704) drove the French from Germany; the Austro-Savoyard victory at Turin (1706) from Italy, and the Anglo-Dutch-Austrian victories at Ramillies (1706) and Oudenaarde (1708) from the Low Countries [37]. However, French victories at Almanza (1707) and Brihuega (1710) won Spain for the Bourbon dynasty [51]. In the War of the Polish Succession (1733–5) the Spanish victory at Bitonto (1734) drove the Austrians from southern Italy, a blow they were never to reverse. Conversely the failure of the Austrians and the French to engage in the Rhineland, where the war was restricted to manoeuvres and sieges (Kehl falling to the French in 1733 and Philippsburg in 1734), prevented any decisive military verdict on their confrontation there. In the War of the Austrian Succession (1740–8) Mollwitz (1741) won Silesia for Frederick II (the Great) of Prussia, a gain consolidated by Hohenfriedberg (1745) [47]. Fontenoy (1745), Roucoux (1746) and Lauffeldt (1747) won the Austrian Netherlands for the French [36], and Piacenza (1746) prevented the Bourbons from conquering northern Italy. These results were as decisive as the crushing of the Highland Jacobites at Culloden in 1746, a battle fought between armies that were armed and trained very differently [34, 67]. During the Seven Years War (1756–63), fought by Austria, France, Russia and Sweden against Frederick II and Britain, there were a number of obvious victories, such as Frederick's defeats of the French and Austrians in 1757 at Rossbach and Leuthen respectively [47] and the Anglo-German victory over the French at Minden (1759), which included a successful infantry advance against cavalry [70].

Parker has argued that 'wars still eternalized themselves ... the Great Northern War endured from 1700 to 1721 in spite of Poltava; the War of the Spanish Succession continued ... in spite of Blenheim, Ramillies, Oudenaarde and Malplaquet' [4:43], but this owed much to their being umbrella wars that comprehended a number of different conflicts – Hanover and Prussia did not attack Sweden until after Poltava – and to the failure to reach negotiated settlements, for example of the Spanish Succession War in 1709–10. The battles themselves were decisive. Turin gave Italy to the Austrians, Poltava gave Livonia to Russia. The armies of the period were more effective than those described by Roberts; the governments better able to sustain wars in which reasonably well-supplied forces could be directed to obtain particular goals, rather than to have to search for food.

The frequently advanced description of eighteenth-century wars as essentially inconsequential, 'wars of limited liability ... fought with limited means for limited objectives' and as characterised by stylised manoeuvre rather than combat, 'a pedantic regard for what had become petrified military rules and conventions ... stabilised complacency' [59:165, 175], is hardly accurate. Though states were obviously limited in their ability to mobilise resources, substantial armies were raised. The Austrian establishment had risen to 165,000 by 1716 while by 1756 the army was about 200,000 strong; in 1783 its complete establishment was 307,000. There were, however, major differences between nominal and effective army strength, differences that reveal the gap between aspiration and achievement in a sphere that was of central concern to the rulers of the period. In 1733 the Austrian army on paper was made up of 153,000 troops but it is probable that the real strength was less than half this [58]. In 1740 the nominal total of Austrian troops was 157,082 but only 107,892 were effective. In 1775 the establishment was 174,645 and effective members were 170,562. Prussian forces, less than 80,000 in 1723, were 150,000 strong in 1757 and rose during Frederick's reign to nearly 200,000. Excluding the Cossacks, the Russian army increased from 200,000 in 1719 to 240,000 in 1740; 344,000 in 1756 and 450,000 in 1795. The Russian field army in 1756 was, however, only 95,000 strong [45]. These efforts, mutually sustained by fear, were not made in order to indulge in a military game. There was tremendous growth in the territories of the Austrian Habsburgs in 1683–1720: Transylvania and most of Hungary (Peace of Karlowitz, 1699); Austrian Netherlands (Belgium and Luxemburg), Lombardy and Naples (Peaces of Utrecht and Rastadt, 1713–14); the remainder of Hungary, northern Serbia and Little Wallachia (Passarowitz, 1718); and Sicily (War of the Quadruple Alliance 1718–20). Such sizeable gains reflected Austria's willingness and ability to fight.

Peter I (the Great) of Russia won and retained in the Great Northern War (1700–21) a Baltic coastline at the expense of Sweden because he proved better able to defeat her than the

Danes and the Saxons, his coalition partners of 1700. Conversely, he failed to win a Black Sea coastline because he was generally unsuccessful in his wars with the Turks (1688–1700, 1710–13), being outmanoeuvred at the river Pruth during his 1711 invasion of Moldavia and forced to negotiate peace at a serious disadvantage. Peter had besieged Azov successfully in 1696, but when he struck closer to the heart of Turkish power he was defeated, because he was simultaneously committed in the Baltic, faced major logistical problems in his campaigns against distant Turkey (as against Persia in 1722–3) and encountered in the Turks a major military power, albeit one that was not developing to any significant extent.

Developments in the late seventeenth century rather than in the period 1560–1660 were responsible for the strength of the major eighteenth-century military powers. There was no simple progression from the years of the putative military revolution, but rather a marked growth in the late seventeenth century to wartime strengths that contrasted with far lower figures for the mid-century combatants. During the reign of Frederick-William of Brandenburg-Prussia (the Great Elector, 1640–88), the army rose from 4,650 in 1640 and, after the end of the Thirty Years War in 1648, 1,800 in 1653 to about 45,000 in the war years of 1672–9 and 30,000 in 1688. Between 1632 and 1680 Russia's active fighting force rose from 35,000 to 129,000. The French army rose from a strength of 70,000–80,000 men in the late 1630s to 85,000 in August 1667 and around 120,000 in February 1672. As with other European forces, the French army expanded in wartime, rising during the War of Devolution with Spain (1667–8) to 134,000, before being cut to 70,000. Louis XIV resolved to increase the army to 144,000 for the attack on the United Provinces in 1672. By the end of the Dutch War in 1678 it had risen to nearly 280,000, about 164,000 of whom served in the field, the largest army in western Europe since that of ancient Rome. Though figures of 400,000 for the army during the Nine Years and the Spanish Succession wars are probably exaggerations, it is clear that the French army was a very substantial force and, although essentially alone, it was able to defy major coalitions during both wars. Though the Spanish army was weak during the reign of Carlos II (1665–1700) and the burden of defending the Spanish Netherlands against French attacks was borne by the Dutch, their German allies and, in the Nine Years War, by the English also, Spanish strength revived under Philip V (1700–46). Though frequently poorly paid, the total size of the army increased to about 80,000, and forces of 30,000 and over 30,000 were sent respectively to Sicily in 1718 and to Italy in 1741–2.

The French were helped by the strength of their fortified places, Vauban's work on the frontier towns between 1678 and 1698 resulting in the construction of 33 new fortresses, such as Arras, Lille, Mont-Louis and New Breisach, and the renovation of many more. Appointed Commissioner General of Fortifications in 1678, he became in 1703 the first engineer to reach the prestigious rank of Marshal of France. In essence his skilful use of the bastion and of enfilading fire represented a continuation of already familiar techniques, and he placed the main burden of the defence on the artillery, but it was the crucial ability of the government to fund such a massive programme that was novel. New Breisach, built to control an important Rhine crossing, cost nearly three million livres to construct between 1698 and 1705. A double line of fortresses was created to defend France's northern frontier [46]. Vauban also systematised siegecraft, showing in the successful siege of Dutch-held Maastricht in 1673 how trenches could march forward by successive parallels and zigzag approaches, designed to minimise exposure to artillery. He also made important advances in the use of mortars in sieges.

Vauban's Dutch counterpart, Menno van Coehoorn (1641–1704), who became Engineer General in 1695, significantly improved Dutch defences and was responsible for a major new fortress at Bergen-op-Zoom. He sought to subject attackers to successive zones of flanking fire, while for the attack he used two new weapons that made high-trajectory fire with explosive bombs effective: the Dutch began to manufacture their own howitzers in the 1690s, while in 1702 a lightweight mortar, the 'cohorn mortar', invented by Coehoorn, was first used, 74 being in use at the successful siege of Kaiserwerth in 1702, about 300 in that of Bonn a year later. Elsewhere major fortifications were constructed and maintained. In 1688 the French envoy in Spain was impressed by the strength and modernity of the citadel at Pamplona. During the personal union of Portugal and Spain (1580–1640) there had been no need to consider the fortresses along the frontier and by 1640 most were totally dilapidated. By 1710, however, after more than thirty years of work, Ciudad Rodrigo was one of the best-fortified towns in Spain. Expensive works were also a feature of the early decades of the following century, the Dutch at Maastricht, the Austrians at Mantua.

If governments could envisage and finance strategic forti-fication systems in the late seventeenth century, it was also possible to create dedicated battle fleets. In the sixteenth and early seventeenth centuries there was increasing professional-isation of naval officers and reliance on specialised fighting ships. As ships were increasingly designed for broadside fire, thus sailing in line-ahead formations, rather than the line-abreast boarding techniques of the previous century, so it became more important to have powerful ships in the line. At the battle of the Downs in 1639, when a Dutch fleet under Tromp destroyed a larger Spanish force, ending an attempt to reinforce the army of Flanders by sea, the attack in line-ahead was first executed in European waters. Whereas before 1642 armed merchantmen had usually composed more than half the English fleet, in the Anglo-Dutch war of 1652–4 they rarely exceeded a third.

The size and firepower of the leading fleets rose, though Spain and Venice both declined as naval powers. Fleets capable of acting at long range were created. As on land, decisive changes, in terms of the size of forces employed and of tactics, occurred in the second half of the seventeenth century. In 1625 the English navy had about 30 ships, in 1640 about 40, in 1651, as a result of a doubling in size under the new Commonwealth government, about 95 and in 1660 about 140. The English fleet was ordered in 1653 to use the line-ahead formation pioneered by the Dutch. The new fighting instruc-tions for the Dutch fleet issued in August 1665 laid down that fighting be done in a single line of battle. In 1666 the signal for forming line of battle was added to the general signal book, thereby completing the adoption of line-ahead tactics by the Dutch navy. The English and the Dutch, who fought three wars between 1652 and 1674, conducted a naval race. In early

1652 the Dutch fleet had 76 ships, and in 1665–7 they built about another 60. The size of the French navy rose substantially in the 1660s and by 1688 the French had a fleet of 93 ships of the line. More important than these numbers were the increases in the size and power of their gunnery. Of the 27 warships built in the United Provinces in 1682–8, 7 were in the 90-gun class. In the following decade the Dutch built 78 ships of 36 guns and over, the English 69 and the French 74.

By June 1757 the British navy had a commissioned strength of 239 ships, of which 90 were ships of the line (ships of 60 or more guns), by 1760 about 300 ships, by 1793 there were 425, and by 1806 over 900 [50]. Though ships of the line were crucial for battles, commerce protection and raiding required lesser-rated frigates and sloops, and between 1714 and 1793 the number of 5th and 6th rates rose from 66 to 114. The British navy was a decisive military force. It was less influential in European diplomacy than was often hoped, but it was instrumental in protecting Britain from invasion on a number of occasions, including 1692, 1708, 1744–6, 1759 and 1805, while it enabled Britain to defeat France in the mid-eighteenth-century struggle for hegemony in North America and to become the dominant European power overseas during the Napoleonic wars [35].

The growth of the Russian fleet dated from the reign of Peter I, though it had been prefigured in the 1660s. A Black Sea fleet of over 50 ships was ready by 1698, the first ship of the Baltic fleet launched in 1703 and over 32 ships of the line were in the Baltic fleet by 1724. In 1700 a special admiralty department was set up, in 1701 a navigation school, and in 1705 recruits were first conscripted specially for the navy, which had hitherto been manned largely by soldiers.

In the same period Peter pushed through the westernisation of the Rusisan army. Western officers, techniques and weapons had been used by his predecessors but never with the system or determination that Peter displayed: 31 new regiments were created in 1699, artillery production was developed on a major scale, a new system of conscription apparently produced over 150,000 men in 1705–9 and military schools were established. As with most of Peter's reforms the results were less impressive than the plans but the defeat of

Charles XII of Sweden at Poltava (1709) and the conquest of the Baltic provinces in 1710 revealed Russia as a leading European military power [45]; a marked contrast to the other major eastern European power that was not always seen as part of the European political system – Turkey. The Turks were defeated by the Austrians at Vienna (1683), Zalánkemén (1691), Zenta (1697), Peterwardein (1716) and Belgrade (1717) [31, 58, 60]. Their mass formations proved increasingly vulnerable to the firepower of disciplined Austrian units. However, the Turkish military system should not be underrated. Austria was defeated in the Austro-Turkish war of 1737–9, and returned Belgrade, northern Serbia and Little Wallachia to the Turks under the Treaty of Belgrade (1739). Under the Kaptan Pasha Mezzomorto (1640–1701) a major revival of the Turkish navy, including the building of a large number of sailing ships at the expense of the traditional galleys, challenged Venetian power, and in 1715 its command of the coastal waters was instrumental in the rapid fall of the Venetian forts in the Morea (Peloponnese region of Greece), one of the most decisive campaigns of the century and one that consisted of sieges with no battle. In 1717 the Turks besieged Corfu, though without success, and southern Italy feared attack. Thanks to their naval revival, Greece remained Turkish and the Aegean remained a Turkish sea, until the challenge of Russian naval power in the Russo-Turkish War of 1768–74, when in 1769 a Russian fleet entered the Mediterranean. This led to the spectacular Russian naval victory of Chesmé (1770), near Chios, when poor Turkish manoeuvring and the use of Russian fireboats resulted in the destruction of the entire Turkish fleet.

In terms of size, weaponry and organisation the major European forces, with the exception of the Turkish and Polish armies, changed more between 1660 and 1710 than in the preceding century. In the following fifty years there were to be other changes, particularly in Prussian recruitment and tactics, though essentially the situation pertaining in 1710 continued until 1740, especially in Austria [58], and it required the shock of defeats in the Austrian Succession and Seven Years wars to galvanise new activity, principally among the Austrians [44] and French respectively. The Austrians feared that their loss of Silesia would be followed, in the next Austro-Prussian conflict, by a Prussian attempt to gain Bohemia. In 1753 a Bavarian official, commenting on the new regulations for the Bavarian army, wrote: 'It is today the hobby of all the major princes'. It could also be found in some of the minor states, the republic of Genoa, for example, reorganising the inspection of her fortifications in 1748.

The changes of 1660–1710 should not be taken as marking the culmination of a supposed earlier revolution, a transfer of tactics and organisation from 'progressive' to other states. This was a factor in Montecuccoli's reforms, but in general there was little continuity with earlier developments. The adoption of the bayonet and the abandonment of the pike was a new development. There was scant continuity with earlier changes in Prussia and Russia, while in Austria, England and France, although there was no abrupt break in 1660 (Montecuccoli and Turenne were not alone in having fought in the Thirty Years War), a more orderly and less financially imperilled domestic context permitted attempts to improve military organisation and strength by new methods. There was now less need to rely on the desperate expedients that had prevailed in the first half of the century, that most unlikely of all periods for the description of administrative revolution, whether it is designated as absolutist, bureaucratic, centralising or military.

# 2 The Limitations of Change, 1660–1760

## (i) Constraints, 1660–1760

Even if historians can accept that major changes did indeed take place over the century from 1600, it is nevertheless the case that warfare continued to encounter many obstacles, ranging from the acute difficulty of operating in the winter to the poor quality of munitions. Technological, economic and social constraints gravely qualify any notion of an early modern European military revolution. The technological constraints remained paramount. At sea there was only a limited amount that could be done with wooden vessels subject to decay and dependent on windpower. Ship performance was depressed by the fouling of hulls, the luxuriant marine growth below water that was a particular problem in tropical waters, along with its kindred problem, attack on timbers by marine worms. The remedy of coppering was applied to the British fleet in the 1770s, though the French did not adopt it until 1785. Poor and unseasoned timber were other major problems, leading to ships being dismasted in storms, and making the supply of top-quality, generally Baltic, naval stores and the denial of them to enemies an important priority of diplomacy and strategy. The role of wind and tide ensured that strategically and politically desirable objectives, such as all-weather blockades or winter operations, were hazardous or impossible. It was with no mere form of words that the Lords of the Admiralty ordered Admiral Sir George Rooke to sail into the Channel in April 1696 'with the first opportunity of wind and weather'. The weather affected both short-range and distant operations. Charles, third Duke of Marlborough, who had commanded the British expedition that decided in June 1758 that St Malo was too strongly fortified to be attacked, commented in October of that year on the failure of the next expedition, whose rearguard had suffered badly when embarking in the face of a superior French force: 'I wish Mr. [General Thomas] Bligh had made the same unalterable determination that I did, which was to trust as little as possible to the winds which all the admirals in Europe cannot command, therefore always to the best of my knowledge to be two days march nearer to my ships than the enemy's army'. The British fleet sent to take Gorée in West Africa from France in late 1758 lost three ships in a gale off the North African coast [80].

On land there was no means of rapid communications for men or supplies. This had serious strategic implications and the difficulty of moving supplies helped to direct operations towards fertile regions such as Lombardy and the Low Countries, which were generally the best defended. Logistical factors were crucial to both strategy and tactics [64]. Armies had to be supplied with fresh recruits, pay, food and munitions. Pay was difficult to provide, but relatively easy to move, being of comparatively low bulk. Food and munitions were bulky and needed in vast quantities. Not only had the men to be fed but also their horses and beasts of burden, such as oxen. Arms and artillery, shot and cannon balls were bulky and heavy, frequently getting stuck in the mud. To move them was not easy. Europe lacked a system of roads, let alone good roads. Instead there were a small number of well-developed routes, such as that from Paris to Lyon or along the northern side of the Apennines from Bologna through Parma, and a mass of tracks of varying quality. Much depended on climate, soil and drainage. Impermeable soils such as clay quickly became quagmires after rain, but even routes on good soils could be hindered by poor drainage, heavy rains and snow melt. Following heavy rain in northern Germany in August 1758 the third Duke of Marlborough wrote 'the foot have marched the last day almost up to their middle in water the whole way'. Bridges were infrequent and many rivers were only crossed by ferry. Wooden bridges and ferries were easy to destroy in wartime. Varying water courses and flooding were problems in, for example, northern Italy. Flooding was a particular problem during the spring thaw, a bad period for campaigning. The roads in eastern Europe were especially bad and this contributed to the marked slowness of the Russian army on the march. Whatever the quality of the route it generally could not stand up to the pressures created by a moving army, and ruts excavated by heavy wagon wheels aggravated the situation still more.

The rivers were not much better. Few rivers had been canalised and many therefore suffered from variable water levels, weirs and tortuous meanders. Many ships had to be towed, never an easy operation in hilly country and numerous rivers were only one-way routes. Waterlogged regions, such as the Danube valley in southern Hungary, were prone to serious disease. In the course of the century canals were constructed in several countries, including France, Prussia and Russia, while Lombardy and the Low Countries possessed relatively good systems of water-borne transportation, but this was not a practical option in most of Europe. In addition winter freeze, spring thaw and summer drought rendered most rivers undependable. In early March 1748 the Duke of Cumberland, commander of the British forces in the Low Countries, reported, 'as yet the rivers are too full of ice to think of embarking the troops from England, as it will be utterly impossible for them to get up the Meuse'.

Thus most supplies had to come by wagon. Long supply trains followed those armies which received their supplies in whole or part from bases or magazines. It was calculated in 1744 that the siege train required by the Allied army in the Austrian Netherlands would 'amount to 10,000 horses and 2,000 wagons', at a cost of £50,000 for six weeks (Bodleian Library MS Eng. Hist. c. 314 f. 46, 51). Those armies which lived off the land had to forage to a very considerable extent. Where a system of contributions had been arranged, by which intimidated areas provided supplies to prevent forcible foraging, troop dispositions had to maintain the basis of fear. Both supply trains and foraging necessitated the detaching of large numbers of troops for protection. Aside from the military consequences, it was commonly the case that forces in the field received inadequate supplies. Insufficient food could lead to mutinous behaviour while poor-quality food affected performance to an extent that the available records leave unclear. Limited preparation, storage and transportation techniques, including the absence of refrigeration, led to much food being spoiled. Poor health was an obvious consequence, though the weakening of those, many already not especially strong, who were not listed as ill might have been more serious in terms of such activities as marching. It was not until 1795 that the issue of fruit juice on ships to deal with scurvy was made official in the British navy and it led to a dramatic fall in the number of sailors sent to hospital.

In 1776–80, during the War of American Independence, only 1,243 of the 175,990 sailors in the British navy were killed whereas 18,541 died of disease. Disease was one of the great problems affecting military life and, though to a lesser extent, operations. It was particularly marked in tropical campaigns, yellow fever being a great killer in the Caribbean [77], but it was also serious in the crowded conditions of ships. The Franco-Spanish attempt to invade Britain in 1779 was crippled as a result. Improvements were made in military medical care, but as the causes and means of transmission of several major diseases were not understood there was a limit to what could be done. The value of ventilated buildings, warm clothing and bedding and adequate food was increasingly appreciated in the barracks that were built in the eighteenth century as civilian billeting became relatively less important, but these facilities were difficult to provide in the field or at sea. Troops on campaign often slept in the open air. Little had been done in this regard even by the Crimean War (1854–6).

Poor conditions were important because desertion remained a major, generally the major, source of troop loss. Conditions were on the whole more orderly in eighteenth-century Europe than they had been in the early seventeenth and in the more regimented societies that constituted the leading land powers desertion should theoretically have been a less serious problem. However, this was far from being the case. The spread of conscription as the major source of recruitment, as it became in Russia under Peter I and in Prussia in 1733 with the introduction of the cantonal system, increased the danger of desertion, whereas the use of volunteers, foreign and domestic, in the smaller early-seventeenth-century armies made it a crucial problem only if pay was deficient, as it frequently was [21], and success lacking.

No solution to the problem of ensuring that a standing army was kept up to strength without continual infusions of new recruits was found during the period, and this ensured that soldiers were often inexperienced and judged unreliable. This in turn encouraged training through drill in infantry tactics that stressed the general firepower contribution of a unit rather than individual shooting. This was further made necessary by the nature of the available weaponry. The weakness of the European industrial base and, in particular, its technological limitations, helped to produce serious problems with the reliability of weapons. The difficulties created by short-ranged weapons, which had a low rate of fire and had to be resighted for each individual shot, were exacerbated by problems associated with poor sights, eccentric bullets, heavy musket droops, recoil, overheating and misfiring in wet weather. As guns were smooth bore and there was no rifling, or grooves, in the barrel the speed of the shot was not high and its direction was uncertain [68]. The calibre of individual Prussian muskets ranged between 18 and 20.4 millimetres, their length varied by up to 8 centimetres. Non-standardised manufacture and wide clearances meant that the ball could roll out if the barrel was pointed towards the ground, while at best the weapon was difficult to aim or hold steady [73]. Cannon were affected by muzzle explosions, defective caps and unexpected backfiring.

There were improvements in the mid-eighteenth century, including the replacement of wooden by iron ramrods (by the Prussians in 1718), and better sights, but the situation remained one of poor individual accuracy for both artillery and infantry. As cannon could not fire indirectly they could not be placed behind cover, but had to be trained directly on their targets. Arms were badly affected by smoke, and after the first shots, battlefield visibility was limited, which put a premium on the fire discipline required to delay shooting until a short range had been reached. Poor visibility also affected command decisions on a number of occasions and in 1758 the third Duke of Marlborough wrote to his wife, 'I must do my duty as a general, keep clear of the smoke and consequently out of shot to see what is going on in order to give proper orders'.

The effects of these problems on operations were considerable. A stress on change and reform, whether on land the policies of Louvois or Montecuccoli, Peter I or Frederick II, or at sea those of the British admiral Anson and the French naval minister Maurepas, can make the period appear one of continual improvement and progressive adaptation. In practice, as with other aspects of government activity, what is striking is both the extent to which policy was reactive – action was taken in response to failure – and the manner in which reorganisation was so often necessary or felt to be so. Military forces proved a good instance of that clash between aspiration and reality which is such an obvious general feature of the administration of the period, possibly, given their importance and the value attached to them, the most crucial instance of all.

*The problem of winter*

Although the ineffectiveness of contemporary administration undoubtedly had serious military consequences, many problems cannot be ascribed to it. One of the most serious was the extent to which land and sea operations generally took place for only half of every year, commonly from April till October. When the grass began growing horses and other beasts of burden could be fed at the roadside. This was important as many armies, such as the Sardinian one operating in Lombardy in March 1734, lacked magazines of dry forage. Even when such magazines existed they could become exhausted, as the British in the Austrian Netherlands discovered in 1744. Their strategy was affected as a consequence, while the attempt to obtain contributions from occupied French territory was unsuccessful, because of the size of the demands. Forage was to be a major problem for the French in the Seven Years War. After the thaw, roads and the land in general were usually reasonably firm until autumnal rains made routes impassable and filled siegeworks with water. Supplies were more plentiful in the late summer, when the harvest had been gathered in, one diplomat writing in May 1747 of the prospect of Frederick II 'attacking Bohemia or his other neighbours, when the forage is upon the ground, and the granaries full'. If troops slept in the field with little or no cover, winter operations could cause major losses through death and desertion. There are many instances of such operations. In the winter of 1674–5 Austrian and other German forces, including Brandenburg-Prussian troops led by the Great Elector, fought a bitter campaign with the French in Alsace. On 27 December 1677 the Swedish fortress of Stettin fell to Brandenburg forces after a long siege, despite the harshness of the winter.

Nevertheless, such operations could be costly and those who pressed for them felt it necessary to defend their views. The Jacobite Sir Henry Goring, arguing for an invasion of England in late 1726, wrote: 'if it should be objected, that to send troops into a foreign country in the winter, they would be liable to great hardships, and that they would suffer very much by keeping the field in that season, the objection is easily answered ... they are going to their friends, who will receive them like their brothers, and make them welcome. They can suffer neither the cold nor hunger, for ... there are no garrisons in England, but a great number of fine open towns.' When Bonnie Prince Charlie invaded England at the end of 1745 his hardy troops were not too badly affected by the weather, but it did prevent Marshal Wade from marching from Newcastle to Carlisle to cut him off and the French from mounting a supporting invasion of southern England, though the role of the British fleet was also important. In late December Wade, ordered to march from Yorkshire to Newcastle 'as fast as the bad roads and this rigorous season will admit of', feared 'we shall reduce our army to nothing by long marches and encampments at this time of year' [34].

The unpredictability of the winter weather affected operations in Italy during the War of the Polish Succession. In 1733–4 good weather allowed the French to cross the Alps and, in alliance with the king of Sardinia, to overrun most of Lombardy, the roads being passable for their artillery. However, by February 1734 snow was hindering the French siege of Tortona and both they and their Spanish allies lost many troops due to winter sicknesses. The following winter the armies remained in their winter quarters, affected by a shortage of money and forage, and by sickness, while spring rain delayed the beginning of the campaign. In late 1742 heavy rain prevented the British forces in the Austrian Netherlands from advancing to attack France, in order to support Maria Theresa of Austria, and a savage winter helped to decimate the French in Bohemia. Bad weather had a more serious effect at sea, where ships could lose their masts, rigging and cables in storms, and be driven aground. Troops moved by sea in the winter generally suffered. In December 1748, when British forces were returning from the Low Countries at the end of the War of the Austrian Succession, the *Scarborough* transport lost a quarter of the horses, while when the *Merry* transport reached Whitby the Secretary at War noted 'the men are very sickly and the vessel has suffered much'.

## Supplies

It was no more possible for eighteenth-century governments to prevent the winter than it was for them to stop the infectious diseases that killed so many troops, helping, for example, in 1735 to defeat the French siege of Austrian-held Mantua, whose extensive water defences were regarded as the source of the fevers that decimated the French. Siegeworks, such as mines to undermine defences, could not be kept dry or rivers unfrozen. However, the rigours of winter operations were exacerbated by supply problems, especially the absence of dry forage, and these problems recur constantly in accounts of eighteenth-century campaigns; for example the Spanish in Italy in 1734 or the British campaigning against France on the Rhine in 1743. Encamped at Spire that October, Lieutenant Colonel Ellison complained of very cold nights and a shortage of provisions and fodder while the Duke of Richmond, a cavalry general, wrote to a leading British minister, Henry Pelham: 'you ask me what we have been doing since Dettingen. The answer is easy, nothing, then you'll say why nothing, to which I will answer ... nothing was prepared such as bread, forage, hospitals etc. to go on with.' Widespread illness and a shortage of heavy artillery were other reasons why the defeat of Franco-Bavarian forces at Dettingen that summer could not be followed up by an invasion of Alsace. That winter both the Austrian and the Spanish armies in Italy suffered considerably from ill health, desertion, and shortages of wood and forage.

Relatively prosperous and organised states had magazine (supply base) systems, as the French did in eastern France, but these were rarely adequate and could be disrupted by retreat. Marshal Saxe's advance in the Austrian Netherlands in 1745–6 deprived the British of their magazines at Antwerp, Brussels and Mechlin. These magazines were of limited value if forces advanced rapidly as the French and British did in Germany in 1741 and 1743 respectively. The advance of Anglo-German forces under the Duke of Marlborough from the Low Countries to the Danube in 1704 in order to release Franco-Bavarian pressure on Austria was a formidable logistical challenge. Depots of supplies were established along the route and the troops were provided with fresh boots. The success of the march forms an instructive contrast to the difficulties that confronted armies making similar rapid advances in the Empire eighty years earlier. Similarly the French invasions of Italy in 1635 and 1733 can be contrasted in terms of logistical provision, while in 1741 the French advanced into Westphalia and the Habsburg hereditary dominions simultaneously in an impressive display of coordinated military power. The greater size of eighteenth-century armies posed formidable logistical problems, especially once conflict had lasted for longer than about two years. Contribution systems (the exaction of supplies on an organised basis) were of only limited use, though they were employed extensively by the Austrians, for example after they conquered Bavaria in the Spanish and Austrian Succession Wars in 1704 and 1742 respectively, and by the Russians in Poland during the Great Northern, Polish and Austrian Succession and Seven Years wars.

Purchasing supplies in the field was made difficult by the limited surpluses of many areas of Europe, especially after a number of campaigns, and by the weakness of government credit, especially in wartime. Despite serving Britain, arguably the wealthiest and most creditworthy of the major states, the Duke of Argyll was obliged to write in June 1711 from Barcelona, where he was commanding forces supporting the claims of the Habsburg candidate to the Spanish crown against his French rival, while allied Spanish troops mutinied for lack of pay and his forces were short of powder and cannon:

> having with greater difficulty than can be expressed found credit to keep the troops from starving in their quarters all this while, which for my part I do not see how we shall be able to do any longer, for the not paying the bills that were drawn from hence the last year, has entirely destroyed her Majesty's credit in this place; but though the troops could be supplied in quarters, that will not now do the business, for the enemy is already in motion . . . so that if we remain in quarters, we shall be destroyed en detaille, and to get together is not in nature till we have money, for the whole body of troops that were here last year are without all manner of necessarys, having both officers and soldiers lost all their tents, baggage and equipages at the battle of Villa Viciosa [10 December 1710], besides that the contractors for the mules to draw the artillery and ammunition and carry the bread will by no means be persuaded to serve any more till we have money to pay them. (Cambridge University Library Add. MS. 6570)

Argyll's letter underlines the crucial role of finance in military operations and the extent to which this posed problems even for as wealthy a state as Britain, which had benefited from the foundation of a national bank, the Bank of England (1694), and the creation of a funded national debt. The serious logistical problems that the armies of the period faced were an important constraint on military operations and constituted a major limitation on the warfare of the period.

*Atrocities*

The exhausted state of belligerents towards the end of and after major wars was both a testimony to the substantial strains that these entailed for countries with weak, predominantly low-productivity agrarian economies, and a cause for governments to desire peace, as the French did in 1709 and 1748. Generals responded to supply problems by altering their dispositions, the Duke of Cumberland explaining one such move in 1757 by: 'The want of subsistence for the troops in the territory of Paderborn that was no longer to be procured there.' Troops often responded by exactions from the civilian population, such as those of the Spanish in the neutral Papal States in 1736 [144]. Accounts of campaigns throw considerable doubt upon the customary picture of post-1648 warfare as having scant effect on civilians. Brutality and destruction were not confined to eastern Europe where religious and ethnic differences appear to have increased human cruelty. In western Europe destruction could be used as a tool of policy, to intimidate or to deny shelter and supplies to opponents, as with the French devastation of the Palatinate and neighbouring parts of Germany in the winter of 1688–9. In the prince-bishopric of Liège, Louis XIV's forces burnt Malmedy and Stavelot and pillaged Huy in 1689, and in 1691 caused a lot of damage in their unsuccessful siege of Liège by the use of heated shot among wooden buildings. When regular forces fought irregulars the fighting was often savage and atrocities were frequent. Examples include the Protestant rising in the Cévennes mountains of southern France in 1702–11 [142], the Tyrolean peasant resistance to a Bavarian invasion in 1703, the subsequent Bavarian peasant rising against Austrian occupiers, the suppression of the Jacobite Highlanders in Scotland in 1746, and the Genoese popular rising that drove out Austrian occupiers in 1746. Soldiers were not trained for irregular warfare and many reacted to it brutally, destroying the homes and crops of peasants in order to wreck their fragile economy. Irregular forces could be very effective, as in the Tyrol and the republic of Genoa, and their major advantages over conventional troops, speed and logistical flexibility, were noted by Lord Glenorchy, a loyal Scottish peer, in March 1746:

the slowness of the motions of so heavy a body as our army gives them opportunities of assembling, separating upon expeditions, and assembling again when they please, hardy people who can sleep sound on the ground, and wet through without catching cold; who can live upon a little oatmeal made into a cake upon a flat stone before a fire in the open air, or mixed with hot water; whose officers can bear the same fatigues ... must have a great advantage over regular forces who must live as well in the field as at home, and whose officers are many of them of delicate constitution.... If the nature of our troops would allow of their being as expeditious as the rebels, they had been scattered long ago.

Fortunately for the regulars in April 1746 the Jacobites did not contest the passage of the Spey, but chose to fight at Culloden, on a battlefield that gave their Highland charge no advantages, after their plan for a surprise night attack on the British camp had miscarried [34].

Atrocities and exactions marked numerous western and central European campaigns in which civilians were not involved. In part this may be attributed to the growing use of light cavalry, the Austrians employing the Hungarians they had raised initially against the Turks in the wars with France and Prussia. The most famous and most feared irregular units were the Pandours and other such forces from the Habsburg military frontier in Croatia. However, defeat, as with the retreating French forces in Germany in 1743, and inadequate supplies also played a major role. The Austrians who invaded the French province of Dauphiné in 1692 ravaged the country and sacked and burnt Gap. In December 1742 Amelot, the French foreign minister, attributed disorders committed by French forces in allied Bavaria to shortages, a similar excuse was made on behalf of Dutch troops in the Austrian Netherlands in 1744, while in 1747 the town of Liège was threatened with plunder unless it made payments to Austrian troops whose pay was in arrears.

*Manpower*

Pay shortages were partly responsible for another problem that vexed Amelot – a shortage of troops. Eighteenth-century governments encountered great difficulties in meeting their manpower requirements, particularly in wartime when wastage rates rose at the very moment that more men were required. In part this reflected their general inability to afford to retain in peacetime forces that would meet wartime demands. This was a major problem for forces that reduced their strength considerably at the end of a war, such as the British army and navy. Disbanded soldiers and sailors often turned to crime, Sir James Kinloch, writing from Barnstaple in January 1759, noting their responsibility for highway robberies. Even if they caused no great social problems they were soon out of training. It was not surprising that the British, like the Dutch and Venetians and, to a lesser extent, the French and Spaniards, felt it advisable when war approached to hire trained foreign units. They were not only thus denied to enemies while freeing domestic workers judged useful, from the dangers of recruitment: hired troops also compensated for the absence of sufficient trained soldiers, in countries that lacked effective systems of conscription or militia that could be drafted into regular units.

However, whatever the size of the army it was necessary to replenish units during wars, because wartime losses, especially through desertion and disease, were considerable. The willingness to recruit deserters exacerbated the situation. Deserters from the French army in Italy in 1734 were recruited by their Spanish allies in Genoa for service in Oran. Prussian deserters often re-enlisted in other Prussian regiments for the sake of bounties. In December 1742 Amelot complained to a French marshal about the difficulty of filling the enormous hole that death and desertion had created in the French army in Germany. The following June he informed Charles Albert of Bavaria that this army had already lost at least half its strength through desertion and illness and that it had been ordered to withdraw to the French frontier: 'the king is absolutely unable to continue such a ruinous war at such a distance ... it is impossible for France to furnish every year a new army from its militia which is sent 200 leagues in order to perish soon after its arrival'. During the Seven Years War the French lost about a fifth of their army annually through desertion, ill health and enemy action, obliging them to find 50,000 replacements every year. Governments responded by recruiting prisoners and deserters and raising troops in the lands of often unwilling allies, as the French did in Zweibrücken in 1743, and of enemies. In 1747 the leading Saxon minister complained that the 5,000–6,000 Saxons forcibly recruited by the Prussians were badly treated. Frederick II forcibly recruited Saxon prisoners again in 1756. Foreigners were often recruited. Italians moved to Spain or Austria, Germans to France, Austria and Russia. In a typical Dutch warship half of the sailors, two-thirds of the soldiers and a third of the petty officers were of foreign origin, mostly from the Empire, Denmark and Sweden. The attempts by minor German princes to win military posts in powerful armies were mirrored by their subjects. One variation of this was the practice of some rulers offering themselves, or more commonly their armies, for the service of other states in disputes in which they had no personal interest, in return for financial benefits. The Landgraves of the German principality of Hesse-Cassel were particularly successful followers of this policy. In 1745 William VIII of Hesse-Cassel compared his army to Spain's South American source of bullion, and declared that without it he would have no resources. The regiments of Royal Allemand, Royal Alsace, Royal Anhalt, Royal Bavière, Royal Deux-ponts and Royal Nassau in the French army brought a steady income to the Catholic princes of southern Germany who allowed the recruitment of their subjects, and served to extend French cultural and political influence in the Empire.

*The Portuguese campaign of 1762*

A case-study of the problems that armies still faced a century after the end of the supposed military revolution is provided by the British expeditionary force sent to Portugal in 1762. This British ally appeared to the Bourbons to be a vulnerable target that could be overrun and exchanged in a general peace treaty for British gains elsewhere. A state of the Portuguese army presented by their government to that of Britain in 1761 revealed that, although in theory the army was 31,000 strong, in fact it only had 16,500 men, while it was short of artillery, horses and supplies. Spanish successes in overrunning weak and poorly defended Portuguese fortresses in early 1762 led to urgent requests for British reinforcements, but these were delayed in the Channel by contrary winds in late June. The following month Brigadier Frederick provided a depressing account of the logistical problems he faced on the march to Santarem, which in part arose from the poverty of the region. Arriving at Porto de Mugen, Frederick had found no beef or bread prepared for his troops and it proved impossible to obtain adequate supplies:

> all the bread that the Magistrate said he could possibly get before they marched was two hundred small loaves which was so small a quantity it was impossible to divide amongst the men. I ordered the regiment to march the next morning at half an hour past three, but the carriages for the baggage not coming at the proper time it was past six before they began their march. It was late in the day before they got to Santarem when Colonel Biddulph reported to me that by the excessive heat and sandy roads that above half the regiment had dropped behind and was afraid many of the men would die, on which surgeons were sent to their assistance. When I arrived at Santerem Lord Allen informed me that the magistrates of that place had told him everything was ready for the troops after which I saw the magistrates, who told me they were then going to the Lower Town to provide for everything against the arrival of the regiment at half past three o'clock. Lieut. Col. Biddulph reported to me that the men were then lying in the streets, the inhabitants had shut up their houses, and the magistrates had provided no quarters for them neither was there beef or bread for the men, and that they were fainting with the heat and want of food.

Clearly the pressure on the soldiers was acute, 'nine men of the Buffs died on the march yesterday' (Huntington Library, Loudoun papers 10125). Frederick's letter lends vivid point to the complaints of British generals over Portuguese supplies, especially of horses, mules, bread, forage and firewood. However, the Spanish failure to exploit their early successes by a march on Oporto had proved decisive, especially in the context of increasingly successful Anglo-French negotiations.

49

Nevertheless, the conflict continued, and the correspondence of British officers throws considerable light on the problems they encountered, especially with communications and in cooperating with the Portuguese. Captain Fraser Folliott reported to the British commander, the Earl of Loudoun: 'I have examined the ford at Belvere over the Tagus situated at Ortiga, and do find five feet water almost all the way over, on the bottom are large rocks and stones, and the current very rapid – I have also been on the other side of the river and find the roads everywhere impassable for wheel carriages.' And later, 'near a third of my company being sick most of them of fevers, if a surgeon's mate could be spared for four or five days he would be of infinite use'.

He wrote to the Count of Schaumburg-Lippe, the commander of the Portuguese army: "Twill be very difficult for me to carry that part of your highness' commands into execution relating to gaining intelligence, without a person who understands the Portuguese and English languages, I've been much distressed already for such a person, and four or five times have I represented this grievance to his Excellency Lord Loudoun' (HL. Lo. 8607, 8604, 8608).

Captain John Ferrier's problems were more mundane. He had had to struggle to construct a durable bridge at Abrantes and he wrote of 'the addition of boats, baulks, and planks, which I was obliged to make at each end of the bridge on account of the excessive rise of the river'. On the other hand Sir James Foulis, given command of a Portuguese regiment at Olivenca, found that he had only 'two battalions that scarcely make up 600 betwixt them, 700 militia and 50 valiant peasants mounted upon mares' (HL. Lo. 10112, 8618).

The correspondence of Loudoun is full of complaint and that was towards the end of a conflict, the Seven Years War, in which the British had acquired considerable experience in overseas expeditions and in relations with allies. Many of the problems, especially the shortage of food and poor communications, reflect the difficulties of operating in a region that was not the most developed or prosperous in Europe, yet it is also clear that the army's ability to cope was limited. Nevertheless, it continued to operate effectively, Burgoyne closing the campaign by storming the entrenched Spanish camp at Villa

Velha successfully. The Bourbon retreat can, in part, be attributed to the start of the winter rains and to the awareness that nothing could be gained in the peace negotiations, but the strength that the British brought to the Portuguese resistance had been important in preventing the Bourbon invasion from being one of the decisive campaigns of the century.

*Conclusion*

Despite the difficulties they faced, forces continued to operate. The Earl of Loudoun's regiment, garrisoning Fort Augustus in the Scottish Highlands, might be short of 1,057 shoes and 1,117 hose in 1747 but similar problems did not prevent other garrisons from continuing. British troops in the Low Countries died from fevers in August 1748 thanks to 'the wetness of this country, the bad stagnated ditch water we drink, the bad food ... we lie in barns and open cowhouses with little or no straw'. But then the Dutch and the French were similarly affected. Problems such as these did not always prevent quick and decisive campaigns. In June 1672 Louis XIV seized the Duchy of Cleves and between the 1st and the 6th simultaneously conducted four successful sieges. In September 1678 Denmark and Prussia conquered the Swedish island of Rügen and began the siege of Stralsund, which fell the following month. The limitations of contemporary military forces did not prevent effective operations, especially if competent leadership and superior strength were present.

The degree to which problems or success, continuity or change should be stressed is, as ever, difficult to determine. No military system has ever been without its problems, but the technological basis of warfare in this period was sufficiently constant to invalidate the description of revolutionary. It was difficult to maintain the impetus in training and to keep standards high. This was but one of the many fields of *ancien régime* government in which legislation, in this case in the issue of new manuals, was of limited effectiveness. Without training it was difficult to benefit from innovations in tactics or weaponry. However, training, particularly if it entailed camps, such as the Prussian summer camps, and manoeuvres, such as those of the Russian fleet in the early 1720s, was expensive and disruptive. As a result there was some-times a lack of interest in it. Many armies only discovered the virtues of preparedness, whether of troops, weaponry, ships or fortifications, when war began. The armed forces of a number of powers did increase in size appreciably and they were used as effective tools of policy, albeit ones that were limited, apart from in conflict with the Turks, by the absence of any substantial technical edge in tactics or weaponry, but their potential was inhibited by a number of serious con-straints that were not to be overcome until the nineteenth century. Then steam-powered iron ships changed the poten-tial of naval power, while land combat was affected by the communications revolution produced by the railway and the telegraph. Infantry firepower rose greatly. These changes were to produce a decisive edge in the struggle of European states to subjugate trans-oceanic societies in the eastern hemisphere and better deserve the designation revolution-ary [78]. It is therefore possible to conclude that no military revolution occurred in post-medieval Europe prior to the nineteenth century, so circumscribed were even the major changes.

## (ii) Limited operations?

*Attack and defence on land, 1660–1760*

That rulers and generals did not wish to lose trained troops on campaign or in conflict did not mean that operations were simply conducted in order to minimise losses. It is true that hand-to-hand infantry fighting was comparatively rare during major battles and was less marked than in the previous century, a consequence of increased firepower and of the demise of the pike. Only 9 per cent of the French soldiers admitted to the Invalides hospital during the Seven Years War had suffered bayonet wounds, while 80 per cent had firearm wounds. However, cold steel remained important in cavalry combat, as it had done so since the early seventeenth century when most cavalry abandoned elaborate pistol drills in favour of swords or lances. Cold steel was also more important in infantry combat than pictures of parallel firing lines might suggest, bayonet charges being employed by Marlborough and Charles XII of Sweden to follow close-range volleys. In the mid-eighteenth century Frederick II, the leading French general Saxe, and the Austrians Khevenhüller and Thüngen extolled cold steel. In 1741 Frederick ordered his infantry to have bayonets permanently fixed when they were on duty and he subsequently introduced a larger and stouter bayonet. This tactic had to be abandoned in 1757 in the face of Austrian defensive positions. The difficulty of combining fire and cold steel harmed Frederick's operations seriously that year, particularly at the battle of Prague. The Prussian army returned to the tactics of firepower, but this did not necessarily reduce casualties, or imply any absence of a desire to win. The exchange of fire between nearby lines of closely packed troops could produce high casualty rates, especially if cannon fire could be brought to bear. One participant on the British side at Dettingen (1743) reported of the French cannon fire: 'Whole ranks were swept off by my side'. In fact the army lost about 2,400 killed and wounded out of 44,000, compared to over 30,000 casualties, besides prisoners, out of the 108,000 combatants at Blenheim (1704), a quarter of the Anglo-Dutch-German force at Malplaquet (1709) and about 13,000 out of 35,000 Prussians when the outnumbered Frederick was defeated by Austrian firepower at Kolin (1757). Many of the generals of the period, such as Turenne, Charles XII, Eugene, Marlborough and Saxe, were determined both to engage in battle and to win, despite these high rates.

*Sieges*

The importance of sieges in many campaigns is frequently cited as cause, example and consequence of the limited nature of operations and the extent to which conflicts were wars of manoeuvre. Investment in fortifications was certainly an appreciable component of military expenditure, particularly of expenditure on new facilities or weapons, though this was an aspect of the average budget considerably less important than pay and provisions. Major efforts were devoted to constructing new or improved fortifications. The Dutch built Fort St Peter with its shellproof chambers at Maastricht in 1701–2, adding in the 1770s the Line of Du Moulin, a complex of dry trenches and bastions with bombproof shelters and mine galleries. After 1713 Victor Amadeus II of Savoy-Piedmont constructed fortresses at great expense to guard the territories gained at the Peace of Utrecht. The late 1720s saw the French carrying out major works at Metz and Thionville, important bases for any invasion of Germany, and the Swedes fortifying the approaches to Stockholm, which had been vulnerable to the raids of Peter I's new Baltic galley fleet, during the latter stages of the Great Northern War. The suppression of the '45 was followed by the construction of Fort St George on the Moray Firth near Inverness, a bastioned fortification that cost over £100,000 and never heard a shot fired in anger.

Aside from these major fortifications, a large number of older works still existed and many towns, such as Utrecht, retained their old walls. The speed and success with which the Duke of Cumberland's artillery battered the defences of Jacobite-held Carlisle castle in December 1745 [34] was ample evidence of the weakness of such works. Parker's argument that new fortification techniques played a major role in causing the military revolution he discerns [4:24–6], fails to tackle adequately the limited extent of the adoption of these techniques. It would be misleading to imply that in general the extent of modern fortifications was anything other than patchy. This was certainly true in Spain, Italy and Germany. In addition, in 1716 a French agent considered Malmo as the only well-fortified place in Sweden, while a British envoy in Brussels wrote: 'I know the frontier towns of this country which are not committed to the care of the Dutch, are in a miserable condition, the fortifications are tumbling down, they have neither ammunition nor provisions in them to sustain 5 days siege.' The poor state of the fortresses on the United Provinces' eastern frontier, such as Delfzyl, crucial in the event of a war with Prussia, was commented on in the mid-eighteenth century.

Parker presents Spain, Italy, the Netherlands and France as 'the heartland of the military revolution', a heartland in which 'the key variable appears to have been the presence of the *trace italienne*' [4:24], but in northern and eastern Europe many campaigns revolved around important fortifications: Russia attacking the Turkish fortresses of Azov, Ochakov and Ismail to the north of the Black Sea; Austria and Turkey struggling to control Vienna, Buda, Temesvar, Belgrade and Orsova. Kamenets-Podolsk was important in the Polish-Turkish struggle for rule over Podolia and the western Ukraine in the late seventeenth century. The Turks took Candia in Crete after a siege of 24 years (1645–69) in which about 100,000 men died, but failed to take Corfu in 1717; and in the Baltic the Swedes struggled to defend Wismar, Stralsund, Stettin, Riga, Reval and Narva from 1655 to 1716. Sieges could act as the focus of campaigns, the Turkish attacks on Russia in 1677 and 1678 centring on unsuccessful sieges of Chigirin. They could delay plans, occupy a large number of troops and require formidable quantitites of supplies, forcing generals to devote more of their resources to protecting their supply lines. The minimum allowance of powder for a serious siege was 700,000 pounds and most authorities agreed that over 1,000 shot were required for each battering piece. Sieges were not inconsequential alternatives to battle. Fortresses performed the crucial strategic function of securing lines of supply and communication, for example along the Danube, across the Rhine or between the Baltic and Black Seas and the great river routes of eastern Europe, and were themselves commonly important supply bases. Fortresses were also significant as a concrete manifestation of control over an area, where armies might otherwise manoeuvre inconsequentially. Fortifications stabilised the inchoate borders of eastern Europe and were the signs and sources of political control in an area of multinational empires and no firm historical boundaries. Fortifications had stabilised the western movement of Turkish expansion and unsuccessful sieges – Vienna (1529), Corfu (1537) and Malta (1565) – blocked her advance in the sixteenth century.

Sieges, such as the unsuccessful French one of Turin in 1706 and the successful Austrian siege of French-held Prague in 1742, played a crucial role in many campaigns. However, sieges were not so important that they commonly dictated the success of conflicts. Though they played a major role in the Spanish and Austrian Succession wars, they were less important in the Seven Years War. Ingolstadt and Ulm fell after the Franco-Bavarian defeat at Blenheim. The successful Russian sieges of Reval, Riga and Vyborg in 1710, which gave her control of Sweden's eastern Baltic provinces, were the consequence of the destruction of the main Swedish field army at Poltava the previous year. Battles not sieges determined the fate of Spain in 1705–10. Military superiority over the Austrians allowed the French Marshal Villars to capture the important Rhineland forts of Freiburg, Kehl and Landau in 1713 [61]. The fate of Danzig (Gdansk) besieged by the Russians in 1734, the crucial military event in the Polish section of the War of the Polish Succession, was sealed when France sent only a small amphibious relieving force and it was defeated. Similarly Saxe's successful manoeuvres and victories in the Austrian Netherlands in 1745–7 were the crucial precondition of his successful sieges, which included Ostend in 1745 and Antwerp in 1746. The Russo-Swedish war of 1741–3, one of the century's decisive wars, was decided by the vigour of the Russian general Lacy, and his larger army. The Swedish fortress of Willmanstrand was stormed in 1741 and the following year the Swedes, outmanoeuvred and shut up in Helsingfors (Helsinki), capitulated [45]. Frederick II concentrated on a war of movement. Fortifications were no substitute for a field army. They could not win a war and in defence they depended on supporting forces. In addition, their maintenance and garrisoning were a considerable burden and, as a result, many were not adequately maintained. In 1733 the chief engineer of the United Provinces inspected the fortifications in the Austrian Netherlands and found them in a poor state of repair, and inadequately garrisoned and supplied. His report is as valuable a comment on the fortifications of the period as the sophisticated defences of strongholds such as Landau, and he was to be proved correct by the French in July 1745, Ghent being invested on the 10th and surrendering on the 15th, Bruges surrendering on the 19th after a two-day siege and Ostend falling the following month.

If sieges could therefore be rapidly successful, it is misleading to imagine that improved defences had made storming impossible. Sieges were an integral part of war; not a soft option; not always decisive; and not to be artificially separated from other military operations. Sieges could also be violent and bloody. The Russians took Ochakov by assault in 1737, Bender in 1770 and Ismail in 1790, the French Prague in 1741 and Bergen-op-Zoom in 1747. A British military official wrote of the siege of the last, 'it has certainly been carried on with great fury by the enemy, without regard to the loss of men and every other expense'. Those who were killed in the streets of the town when it fell would no more have appreciated being told that they lived in an age of limited war than the Prussian soldiers in the Seven Years War, who had only a 1 in 15 chance of survival. Louis XIV and some of his ministers and generals may have come to prefer caution, the concentration of massive forces to ensure predictable success in sieges, but their policies should not be regarded as typical.

### (iii) Colonial conflict

Parker has correctly identified shifts in the political relationship between Europe and the outside world as one of the most important consequences of European military developments [4:115–45]. This was made increasingly clear in the post-1660 period by the decline of Turkey as a military power. The Turks were still a major military power in the eighteenth century [84] able, helped by limited Austrian resources and poor generalship, to defeat the Austrians in 1737–9 [87], but their continued use of undifferentiated charges by mass formations was increasingly vulnerable to the greater firepower of disciplined European units. In 1782 a French general discussing how to capture Gibraltar remarked, 'his idea was to proceed à la Turque, to sacrifice men, maintaining that no place however strong could resist that kind of attack'. However, the Turks were no longer successful. In 1781 Frederick II noted that they needed to improve their artillery and increase the discipline of their troops. Defeats at the hands of Austria and Russia in 1787–91 led Selim III (1789–1807) to seek French assistance in improving his forces [89]. In North

Africa which, with the exception of independent Morocco, was under at least the nominal authority of Constantinople, Spanish attacks on Algiers in 1775, 1783 and 1784 were repelled and Spain forced to buy peace in 1785; while Oran, lost by Spain in 1708 and recaptured in 1732, was evacuated in 1792; though in 1798 Napoleon's victory at the battle of the Pyramids was followed by the temporary conquest of Egypt. The British subsequently defeated the French there, but neither power was able to maintain a presence and Britain did not gain control of Egypt until a successful invasion in 1882 and the battle of Tel-el-Kebir. Superior firepower and disciplined troops played a major role in Clive's victory over superior Indian forces at Plassey (1757) which made the British *de facto* rulers of Bengal, the province that was to serve as the centre of their power in India.

However, the impact of European states on Asia was limited in this period. The Turks pushed back against Portuguese advances in the Persian Gulf and Red Sea in the sixteenth century; the Omanis captured Muscat from the Portuguese in 1650 and Mombasa from them in 1698; the Russians had to abandon their gains in Persia in 1732; and little was gained at the expense of China. In 1689 Russia ceded the Amur valley to China by the treaty of Nerchinsk, a loss that was not reversed until 1858. Between 1680 and 1760 the Manchu dynasty also conquered Taiwan, Outer Mongolia, Tibet, eastern Turkestan, Tsinghai and south-eastern Kazakstan, a formidable amount of territory that brought rule over a large number of non-Chinese peoples. Though the Russian Cossacks had, thanks to their firearms, overrun thinly-populated Siberia from the 1580s, founding Okhotsk on the Pacific in 1648 [86], and this advance was subsequently consolidated in the eighteenth century, with the additional gain of the Kamchatka peninsula and the southern coast of Alaska, the military strength of the local people ensured that Russian penetration of central Asia remained limited. The Kazakh nomads to the east of the Caspian were nominally vassals, but the area was not fully dominated militarily until the 1850s. The Khanates of Bukhara, Khiva and Kokand were not to be conquered until after 1860. Though the Crimea was finally subjugated as a result of the superiority of Russian numbers, firepower and fortifications over the Tatars, and was annexed in 1783, the Russian impact in the Caucasus was limited [81]. Louis XIV's intervention in Siam (Thailand) was unsuccessful, and both the British and the French were defeated when they sought to benefit from the Burmese civil war in the 1750s. In 1737–40 Goa, the centre of Portuguese power in India, was involved in a disastrous war with the Maratha confederation. It would be wrong to think of the struggle between European and Asiatic powers as the central military development of the period in Asia. The greatest battles in the eighteenth century were still waged between Asiatic powers, for example the victory of Nadir Shah of Persia over the Mogul Emperor of India, Muhammad Shah, whose army was estimated by contemporaries to be 200,000 strong, at Karnal in 1739 or the Afghan defeat of the Marathas at Panipat in 1761. Russian relations with Turkey and Persia in the 1720s must be seen in the context of the major war between the two latter powers which lasted until 1748 [84]. Tongking (Vietnam) conquered Cochin China, Burma and Arakan, though it failed to gain Siam, and China launched abortive invasions of Burma and Tongking. It was not until the following century that the European powers came to dominate Asia and Africa.

European military techniques did not always prove appropriate to colonial fighting conditions. The British governor of Jamaica, unsuccessfully fighting the Maroons, runaway slaves, reported in 1738: 'The service here is not like that in Flanders or any part of Europe. Here the great difficulty is not to beat, but to see the enemy ... in short, nothing can be done in strict conformity to usual military preparations, and according to a regular manner; bushfighting as they call it being a thing peculiar by itself.' In 1738–9 the Maroons were granted land by treaties. The native Caribs retained their position in northern St Vincent and resisted an attempt to extend British plantations there in 1771–2. In 1755 the force of regulars sent under General Braddock to establish British power in the Ohio river region disputed with France was defeated near Fort Duquesne by the French and their Indian allies, who made excellent use of tree cover to fire at the exposed British force, whose morale collapsed in the face of the novel challenge. Lieutenant-Colonel Thomas Gage reported:

> a visible terror and confusion appeared amongst the men.... The same infatuation attended the whole; none would form a line of battle, and the whole army was very soon mixed together, twelve or fourteen deep, firing away at nothing but trees, and killing many of our own men and officers. The cannon were soon deserted by those that covered them. The artillery did their duty perfectly well, but, from the nature of the country, could do little execution ... the enemy always giving way, whenever they advanced even on the most faint attack.... I can't ascribe their behaviour to any other cause than the talk of the country people, ever since our arrival in America – the woodsmen and Indian traders, who were continually telling the soldiers, that if they attempted to fight Indians in a regular manner, they would certainly be defeated ... the only excuse I can get from them is, that they were quite dispirited from the great fatigue they had undergone, and not receiving a sufficient quantity of food; and further, that they did not expect the enemy would come down so suddenly.

Horatio Sharp, the Governor of Maryland, suggested that 'in case of another campaign against Fort Duquesne ... there ought to be two, or at least one, thousand of our woodsmen or hunters, who are marksmen and used to rifles, to precede the army and engage the Indians in their own way' [80: I, 209–21].

In 1776, when the enemy were American rebels who had just been driven from Canada, a British officer wrote: 'The war in this country is only fit for savages and robbers, it must be all carried on in woods, it is a *Petite Guerre*, proper to make good partisans, and the best qualification for a general is to be a good commissary to supply the army with provisions or a good mechanic to build batteries etc.'

In fact a lot of the fighting in North America was a position warfare of a familiar type, as around New York in 1776, and the weapons used were familiar ones. Nothing came of the suggestion made in 1776 by Benjamin Franklin to Charles Lee, a Major-General in the Continental Army of the American rebels, that bows and arrows should be used, though it throws light on some of the problems that muskets entailed:

> I still wish, with you, that pikes could be introduced, and I would add bows and arrows. These are good weapons not wisely laid aside:
> 1. Because a man may shoot as truly with a bow as with a common musket.
> 2. He can discharge four arrows in the time of charging and discharging one bullet.
> 3. His object is not taken from his view by the smoke of his own side.
> 4. A flight of arrows, seen coming upon them, terrifies and disturbs the enemy's attention to their business.
> 5. An arrow striking in any part of a man puts him *hors du combat* till it is extracted.
> 6. Bows and arrows are more easily provided everywhere than muskets and ammunition . . . .
> If so much execution was done by arrows when men wore some defensive armour, how much more might be done now that it is out of use.
> (*Diplomatic Correspondence of the United States* II, 69–70)

The American War of Independence demonstrated the importance of factors that were to be crucial in European trans-oceanic conquests the following century. Substantial forces operating at a considerable distance had to be supplied, and armies had to adapt to different tactical problems, including irregular warfare, and wide-ranging operations [74, 79, 82, 85, 88, 90, 91]. The American rebels had a local base, but in trans-oceanic conflict between European powers control of the sea was crucial, because supplies and reinforcements generally came from the home country. Nevertheless, naval dominance was not sufficient, as the British discovered in their attacks on Spanish Caribbean possessions, especially the unsuccessful Cartagena expedition of 1741, and on French Canada and the French West Indies [77]. It proved difficult to master the problems of amphibious warfare, the ravages of disease discouraged siege operations in the Caribbean and the Spanish local defence arrangements in the New World proved generally successful. Trans-oceanic operations were most victorious when directed at trading stations that lacked a hinterland on which they could rely for support, for example those in West Africa.

War between the major European colonial powers ensured that their trans-oceanic operations were largely directed against each other in the seventeenth and eighteenth centuries, as with the British capture of Spanish-ruled Havana and Manila in 1762. After 1815 the situation changed, and rivalry was to be expressed by seizing territory not hitherto ruled by Europeans, a process that was to be facilitated by the introduction of steamships and steel artillery.

## (iv) The coming of revolution

It was far from the case that from 1792 a static *ancien régime* military system was confronted and overcome by the armies of revolutionary France. Apart from the defeats that the revolutionary forces suffered, such as Neerwinden (1793) and Amberg (1796) at the hands of Austria [102], and the importance of elements of the royal army in these forces [103], the *ancien régime* military situation was far from static. Some armies appeared inflexible. Earl Cornwallis, who had had to surrender his outmanoeuvred and isolated army to George Washington at Yorktown in 1781, attended the Prussian military manoeuvres in Silesia four years later. He wrote: 'The manoeuvres were such as the worst General in England would be hooted at for practising; two lines coming up within six yards of one another, and firing in one another's faces till they had no ammunition left: nothing could be more ridiculous.' Prussian lack of success in the War of the Bavarian Succession (1778–9) owed something to the mental and physical failings of the aged Frederick II, a failure that illustrated one of the problems of autocratic leadership – physical decline – as serious, if not as spectacular, a disadvantage of the monarchical state as the uncertainties created by the issue of succession. One sign of Frederick's somewhat anachronistic attitudes was his preference for the cavalry over the artillery, where he sent the worst recruits and which he failed to provide with a proper command structure; in its way a failure as serious as his delay in grasping the possibilities of light infantry. Frederick made changes in response to the improvements of his enemies, but they could not compensate for the loss of the comparative military advantage he had enjoyed over his neighbours in the 1740s. That window of opportunity had enabled him to win and hold Silesia. Once it was lost, the discrepancy in resources between Prussia and her enemies placed her in a very difficult situation, forcing her to rely on diplomatic skill. When this proved inadequate, as in Frederick's last years, Prussia found herself isolated, forced to respond to the initiatives of Austria and Russia. The alliance of these powers was too formidable, and Prussia's attempt to challenge it in 1790–1 had to be abandoned. Despite his threats Frederick William II could not risk war.

In general the decades after 1763 were spent in digesting the lessons of the Seven Years War, particularly by the French, who had been humiliated by defeat. There was considerable interest in the use of light infantry and cavalry [94, 98]. Light infantry, trained to operate in open order rather than in ranks and after 1750 armed generally with rifles, were a flexible force that could play a crucial role in skirmishing. Firing individually, not by volley, they could be effective on the battlefield. Light infantry became an established feature of the British army during the Seven Years War.

The French adopted the division, in theory a self-sufficient force, as the basic administrative unit in 1787–8, though this proved difficult to follow in field operations and did not become standard until 1796 [99]. Their army was re-equipped with a new musket and, thanks to Gribeauval, with more mobile and accurate artillery [68: 15–36] and there was considerable discussion of the virtues of attacking in mobile columns in place of linear tactics. These columns were to be found effective when, from 1791, the French Constituent Assembly having decreed an army and reserves of about 250,000, the army was enlarged by a mass of inexperienced citizen soldiers. By the autumn of 1794 its theoretical size was

1,169,000, its real size probably 730,000, the largest army France had ever fielded. This increase in size was crucial in enabling France to resist its opponents. The Prussian army that invaded France in 1792 turned back at Valmy in the face of a larger force, being outnumbered by about 35,000 to 59,000. Later that year at Jemappes an Austrian army of 13,200 was defeated by a French force of 45,000 and the Austrian Netherlands were overrun [92, 93, 95, 96]. Other radical political movements had been overthrown by *ancien régime* armies, the Dutch Patriots by the Prussians in 1787, those in the Austrian Netherlands and the bishopric of Liège by the Austrians and Prussians, the Poles by the Prussians and Russians in 1794 and the Irish by the British in 1798. Radical fervour and the notion of a people's war were no guarantee of military success. France was not united against its foreign enemies, but riven by civil division and conflict as Poland had been in earlier episodes of apparent popular national unity against a foreign foe, such as the anti-Russian Confederation of Bar in 1768. However, the vigorous and uncompromising response of the Parisians to domestic opponents and the failure of the latter to unite behind a common strategy settled the fate of France, while her foreign foes were diverted in the crucial early years of the war by the interest in and concern about the fate of Poland, which was partitioned for a second time in 1793 and a third, destroying her independence, in 1795. In 1735 and 1748 Russian troops had moved towards the Rhine in order to block any danger of the French overrunning Germany. In 1794, however, Suvorov's army was storming Praga, creating in that suburb of Warsaw scenes of carnage reminiscent of the worst outrages in the Thirty Years War.

Nevertheless, revolutionary, and still more Napoleonic, France was a formidable military force. Though its tactical methods were not revolutionary and it suffered from the same technological constraints as its rivals, the scale of warfare it provoked was novel [97, 101]. The domestic context in France is in some respects reminiscent of the urgency, energy and determination with which Peter the Great had tried to change Russian society under the impetus of initial defeat at the hands of Sweden, but French developments in the 1790s were not dependent on one man. The Revolution created an officer-class dominated by talent and connections rather than birth and connections. The revolutionary military effort was in part supported by exactions from conquered areas, but the reorganisation of French society also produced more resources. It was, however, a reorganisation based on necessity, and the forceful implementation of an ideology. This would have been and was unacceptable to societies that, albeit largely within a narrow elite, relied on a consent that was no less important because it generally lacked constitutional expression.

# 3   Military Change and European Society

I am delighted to hear that you found your regiment in such good order. Soldiers are the pillars of the state. If they are not maintained with a continual attention to the order and excellent condition that they should be in the state will be threatened with ruin and the first storm will overthrow it.

(Frederick II to his brother Prince Henry, 1751, *Politische Correspondenz Friedrichs des Grossen*, 8, 488)

## (i) Absolutism and military change

Rather than presenting the absolutist states of late-seventeenth-century Europe as the products of military change, the new-found strength of new model armies, as scholars influenced by the Roberts' thesis have been inclined to do, it is possible to reverse the relationship. By setting the decisive changes, in terms of size and, though to a lesser extent, organisation and weaponry, in the post-1660 period it can be argued that it was the more stable domestic political circumstances of most states in that period, which contrasted notably with the civil disorder of so many countries in what has been termed the mid-seventeenth-century crisis [106, 117, 127], that made these changes possible. Such a revision requires, however, a new explanation of these circumstances, one that no longer relies on military strength. Instead, it is possible to stress stability rather than order, consensus rather than coercion, government as a part of elite society, rather than an external force seeking to mould it. The nature of absolutism can be defined as a politico-social arrangement,

67

rather than a constitutional system, by which the social elite was persuaded to govern in accordance with the views of the ruler, while these views were defined in accordance with the assumptions of the elite. This, indeed, was the essential basis of early modern European political organisation but it had been challenged in the sixteenth century by the division of western Christendom in the Reformation. That had destroyed the bonds of obedience, good kingship and mutual respect that had held rulers and nobles together, replacing them with the stark division of heresy. As rulers were pledged to defend the faith and correctly regarded any threat to the religious homogeneity of their possessions as likely to sap obedience and thus as treasonable, an attitude encouraged by the growing power of sixteenth-century rulers, both Catholic and Protestant, in church affairs, it was not surprising that the Reformation wrecked the domestic peace of much of Europe.

*Sixteenth-century disorder*

The Reformation had least effect in countries that remained or became relatively homogeneous, Catholic Iberia and Italy and Protestant Scandinavia, but in the British Isles, France, the Low Countries, the Empire, Poland and the Austrian Habsburg territories, the result was division and civil strife. Theirs was a political world of conspiracy, the search for assistance from foreign co-religionists and regional, social and factional differences exacerbated by confessional antagonism. It was a political world in which everything was seen to be at stake because of the prospect of state-directed religious change. Peasants revolted against their lords, as in Austria in 1594–7, rulers were assassinated, two successive kings of France, Henry III and IV being killed in 1589 and 1610, or removed by revolt, as Mary Queen of Scots was in 1568, and royal deaths were plotted, as Elizabeth I of England's was on several occasions.

The international consequences were striking. The Emperor, Charles V (1519–58), who inherited the Austrian Habsburg, Aragonese, Castilian and Burgundian inheritances, had been told in 1519 by his Grand Chancellor Gattinara, 'God has set you on the path towards a world monarchy'. French hostility and the advance of the Turks, who overran Hungary in 1526 and besieged Vienna in 1529, affected Charles, but it was the opposition of the Protestant princes that fatally weakened his power as Emperor. In 1531 they created the Schmalkalden League to defend Protestantism and, after attempts at religious reconciliation at the Diets of Augsburg (1530) and Regensburg (1541) had failed, Charles, with Spanish troops, defeated the Protestants at Mühlberg (1547), only to be driven from Germany in 1552 by the French-supported Protestants. By the Peace of Augsburg (1555) Lutheranism was recognised and Lutheran princes allowed to convert their territories to Lutheranism. Imperial authority was fatally compromised.

The Valois kings had united France around the dynasty in the fifteenth century, defeating the English and the dukes of Burgundy, and had then played an aggressive international role, beginning the Italian wars in 1494. However, the French Wars of Religion, which broke out in 1560, led to a collapse of royal authority, foreign intervention, especially by Spain and England [16], and social strife. The period of the wars, which lasted until 1598, resuming during the reign of Louis XIII to end with royal victory in 1629, was not uniformly chaotic. The years 1577–84 were relatively peaceful, but by the end of 1588 Henry III had been driven from Paris by the Catholic League, obliged to recognise their candidate, the Cardinal de Bourbon, as his heir and had to note the hostile speeches of their supporters at the Estates General at Blois. The fortress of Saluzzo had also been taken that year by Charles Emmanual I, Duke of Savoy. Henry's desperate response, the murder of the League leader the Duke of Guise in Blois in December 1588 and the arrest of Bourbon, did not solve the problem. Instead the League turned against the Crown, whose power was soon restricted to a section of the Loire valley. Paris did not return to royal authority until 1594 and the League was not dissolved until 1596 [132]. As a result of religious divisions, both England and Scotland faced conspiracy, such as the Catholic Ridolfi (1571–2), Throckmorton (1582) and Babington (1586) plots aimed at replacing Elizabeth I by Mary Queen of Scots; insurrection, such as the rising by the Protestant Sir Thomas Wyatt against the Catholic Queen

Mary of England in 1554; and foreign intervention, such as Elizabeth I's successful military intervention in Scotland in 1560 on behalf of the Lords of the Congregation, a noble faction, inspired by anti-French sentiment, Protestantism and opportunism, to rebel in 1559 against Mary of Guise, the French-backed French Regent for Mary Queen of Scots, then wife of Francis II of France. Philip III of Spain sent troops to Ireland in 1601–2 to help the rebellion against Elizabeth. Two pregnant developments, the union of the crowns of Poland and Sweden in 1587, when Sigismund Vasa of Sweden was elected king of Poland, and the joining of one of the wealthiest regions of Europe, the Low Countries, to Spain, were ended by politico-religious strife. The Polish-Swedish union was broken in 1598 when Sigismund's uncle Charles seized power in Sweden and Sigismund's invasion of the country was unsuccessful [131]. In the Low Countries fighting broke out in 1566 and in 1581 the States General renounced their allegience to Philip II [20, 126].

Confederations and rebellions were not alien to the nature of sixteenth-century political society. They reflected explicit and implicit theories of noble constitutionalism and contractualism, of obedience to a ruler in return for his good kingship, his fair disposal of patronage. Essentially such behaviour was designed to seek not the overthrow of kingship but its restoration from the influence of evil advisors and pernicious policies, and it commonly led to compromise and reconciliation. Religious division made such reconciliation impossible by destroying the basis for compromise. When in 1577 the Spanish Governor General in the Netherlands, Philip II's illegitimate brother, Don John, signed the Eternal Edict with the States General, promising to send away the unpopular Spanish troops, the provinces of Holland and Zeeland rejected the stipulated restoration of Catholicism, recalled their delegates from the States General and refused to recognise Don John's authority. In 1579 the Walloon nobles of the Union of Arras, who were Catholics, came to similar terms with Philip II, who had to promise to govern with the consent of the Estates, but these were again rejected by the Protestants.

An inability to compromise led to conflict, interrupted only by periods of uneasy truce and exhaustion. The Edict of

Nantes of 1598, by which the French Huguenots (Protestants) extorted limited rights to worship and the garrisoning of about 100 strongholds, was not a satisfactory solution to the French Wars of Religion and religious conflict resumed in the 1610s and 1620s [125]. The Twelve Year Truce that brought peace to the Low Countries in 1609 did not turn into a permanent peace. War between Spain and the Dutch resumed in 1621. It proved impossible to devise lasting acceptable settlements to the religious problem in the territories of the Austrian Habsburgs, Austria, Bohemia and Christian Hungary. The Letter of Majesty which Rudolf II was obliged by the rebellious Estates of Bohemia to sign in 1609, giving the Bohemians the right to be Protestant and allowing the construction of Protestant churches and schools, was an agreement extorted by pressure, the levy of troops by the Estates, as was that made the same year by his brother Archduke Matthias granting the Protestant nobles and towns of Austria full religious liberty. The unstable nature of the politico-religious settlement in the Habsburg lands led to armed confrontation and conflict on a number of occasions, culminating in a revolt in Bohemia in 1618 that led the following year to the deposition of Matthias' heir Ferdinand of Styria as king and the offer of the throne to the Calvinist Elector Palatine Frederick V. This breakdown of Habsburg authority was more complete than earlier episodes and it led to the so-called Thirty Years War (1618–48) [22]. The process of devising an acceptable settlement was most successful in Poland where the Confederation of Warsaw of 1573 guaranteed full religious freedom, especially to the nobility. With its substantial Orthodox population, religious heterogeneity was already established in Poland, and the absence of strong central authority encouraged diversity.

*Seventeenth-century redefinition*

The first half of the seventeenth century saw a process of religious definition, as conflicts which confessional differences either helped to cause or in which they played a major role led in the 1620s to the political collapse of Protestantism in the Habsburg lands, bar Hungary, and in France. Following the victory of the Catholic League over the Bohemians at the White Mountain outside Prague in November 1620, one of the most decisive battles of the century, Catholicism and Habsburg authority were firmly established in Bohemia and Moravia. Upper Austria, which had supported Frederick's cause, was overrun in 1620, and the Protestant revolt that the process of Catholicisation provoked in 1626 was put down. The Huguenot stronghold of La Rochelle was besieged successfully in 1627–8 by a French army commanded by Louis XIII and the English attempt under the Duke of Buckingham to relieve the city was repulsed. The Huguenot rebellion ended with the grace of Alais (1629), the Huguenots retaining their religious privileges but losing their military strongholds [125]. The Huguenots took no part in the *Fronde*, the civil wars of 1648–53 caused by Parisian and aristocratic opposition to the position and policies of Cardinal Mazarin, the dominant minister during Louis XIV's minority. A lasting German religious settlement, the Peace of Westphalia (1648), was produced by the Thirty Years War and the same peace brought recognition of Dutch independence and of the Protestant failure to conquer the southern Netherlands, which the Dutch had sought to do. The British civil wars of 1638–51, which were in large part wars of religion, resulted in a significant worsening of the Catholic position in Ireland. This deteriorated further after the Catholic defeat at the hands of William III of Orange in the war of 1689–91 that followed his successful invasion of England in 1688. The Protestant position deteriorated in Poland. In 1668 conversions from Catholicism were prohibited under pain of exile. In 1673 Protestants were banned from admission into the nobility.

These changes were accompanied by and resulted in a large-scale movement of the nobilities of the regions concerned away from the defeated religion, which essentially became the disadvantaged faith of disadvantaged people. In 1625 the people of Upper Austria were ordered to attend Catholic worship by the following Easter or leave, the nobles being allowed fifty years to convert. There were widespread conversions of Protestant nobles to Catholicism in France, in the Habsburg lands (a process that had begun in the 1590s), and in Poland: many of those who would not convert went into exile, as Catholic nobles did from Ireland in 1691, the rest sinking into rural passivity, cut off from royal patronage and political importance, as the British and Dutch Catholics were. It was this process that was crucial to the enhanced domestic stability of late-seventeenth-century states, and it led to a renewal of crown–elite cooperation and, in reaction to recent problems, to a new stress on order, political, religious and social. The conversion of the Huguenot nobility eased the path for the revocation of the religious concessions in the Edict of Nantes, which was announced in the Edict of Fontaine-bleau (1685).

This ideological cohesion was more important than the supposed common interest in oppressing the peasantry and controlling the towns that has been seen as the central characteristic of absolutism [105]. Clearly there were shared interests and cooperation led to financial benefits in terms of taxes for the crown and exemptions and privileges for the nobility [107], but it is important not to exaggerate the social cohesion and common purpose of the nobility, or the threat posed by the peasantry. Political considerations were crucial to relations between monarchs and leading nobles and these centred on issues of factional benefit within nobilities that were articulated by competing patronage networks [124], and thus divided, rather than united, by common social interests. There were of course other pressures and these can be seen in the supposed mid-seventeenth-century crisis. A sense of regional-national consciousness was crucial in the Catalan and Portuguese rebellions of 1640 [114, 115]; while the strains classically placed upon crown–elite relations, specifically patronage, during a royal minority, played a major role in the *Fronde*, as they had earlier done in civil conflict in France in the 1610s, during Louis XIII's minority and adolescence, and were to do in creating instability in Russia during the regency of Sophia (1682–9) and the reigns of the young Peter II (1727–30) and Ivan VI (1740–1).

The revival of consensus owed much to the resolution of and accommodation to the crises of the mid-seventeenth century, but these specific political achievements have to be balanced with longer term trends, especially the creation of ideological cohesion through the extirpation or political marginalisation of aristocratic religious diversity. The role of political conjunctures was clearly important, as can be seen by contrasting the *Fronde* with the generally peaceful minority of Louis XV (1715–23), when serious divisions over the composition of the ministry, foreign policy and relations with the Papacy were handled without a breakdown of government and order [134]. Similarly, the succession of competent adult male rulers helped to keep Brandenburg-Prussia politically stable from the accession of Frederick William I (the Great Elector) in 1640, and also Savoy-Piedmont in the eighteenth century, after the regencies following the accessions of Charles Emmanual II in 1638 and Victor Amadeus II in 1675 [136]. However, it is also important to appreciate that civil conflict was not generally sought and that the revival of crown–elite cooperation helped to alter the context of political disputes in most countries. The relationship was not always an easy one as monarchs, driven in part by financial exigencies, many of which derived from war, sought to cope with problems. In the second half of the eighteenth century the situation was exacerbated by a growing impatience with many, though by no means all, inherited privileges that characterised the rule of the so-called Enlightened Despots [109, 110]. The Emperor Joseph II (1780–90), who attacked privilege most comprehensively and faced in the Austrian Netherlands and Hungary possessions with a strong consciousness of autonomy, provoked risings in both, but these difficulties were exceptional. His fellow 'despots' maintained crown–elite cooperation, while Joseph's successor Leopold II (1790–2) was able to restore order relatively easily.

The continued problems that the Habsburgs faced in Hungary in the late seventeenth and early eighteenth centuries, culminating in the Rakoczi rebellion of 1703–11 [142], indicated the difficulties that a nobility with a sense of distinct political and religious privileges could create in the absence of harmony with the crown. Royal power in Hungary was not to increase appreciably until the reigns of Charles VI (1711–40) and Maria Theresa (1740–80) brought a measure of such cooperation. Stability in Britain was challenged when the monarch, the Catholic James II (1685–8), moved away from Protestant consensus, leading to domestic conspiracy, foreign invasion, dynastic coup and constitutional change, the Glorious Revolution of 1688, and consequently to civil war in Scotland and Ireland [40]. Harmony was restored with difficulty. After William III's successes in Ireland in 1690–1 most of the Catholic leaders of society emigrated and the political order was based on the Protestant Ascendancy, the Anglican landowners with their Dublin Parliament cooperating with the representatives of the London government. In Scotland a new order, with Presbyterianism as the established church, excluded not only the Catholics but also the far more numerous Episcopalians, and support for the exiled Stuarts among these groups fuelled risings, largely in the Highlands, in 1715 and 1745. In England and Wales there was less resistance to William and, after 1714, to the new Hanoverian dynasty, although the extent of enthusiasm for them was limited. Nevertheless, both Parliament and the government, both central and local, secular and religious, were dominated by the nobility and their relatives and dependents. The religious settlement of 1688–9, in which the exclusion of the Catholic James was central, ended several decades of uncertainty over the position of the Church of England. This served as a basis for the development of new constitutional relationships between crown and Parliament and for a less volatile political situation. English politics were contentious, and the fundamental stability of the system was challenged by the existence of a Stuart claim to the throne, but compared to the political world of 1678–88 – the years of the Popish Plot (1678) and the Exclusion Crisis (1679–81), the Monmouth rising (1685) and the Glorious Revolution (1688) – that after 1689, and especially after the consolidation of Whig hegemony in 1716–21, was more settled.

If the reconciliation of crown and elites brought new political stability to many states, including crucially France [118, 124] and Austria [116], it also had important military consequences. It is not surprising that the two most effective military powers in the early seventeenth century, Spain and Sweden, were both relatively stable domestically. The importance of such stability, crucial to the flow of money and credit on which military operations depended, rose in the second half of the century as the armies of the major powers grew in size and the proportion of natives in the ranks rose. Rulers lacked the administrative resources to govern except in cooperation with the social elite [121] and that was what they sought to do, to the mutual benefit of both. Much-trumpeted administrative innovations, such as the French *intendants*, tended to be weak and often *ad hoc* commissioners and expedients, and dependent for their success on cooperation with the local elites. Far from being intended to replace or circumvent officials who were unreliable, the *intendants* were initially designed to assist the *gouverneurs*, provincial governors who were generally leading aristocrats. Apparently centralised and bureaucratic new-model governments and institutions [133] dissolve under scrutiny into parts of the already comprehensive patronage structures of society conducting their affairs inefficiently in an essentially pre-statistical age. The major attempt to break with the past, that of Peter I (1682–1725) in Russia [128, 130], was less dramatic than it appeared. Many of the institutions and practices he created and fostered proved weak or short-lived and the traditional nobility dominated the first four ranks of the socio-governmental hierarchy defined by the Table of Ranks issued in 1722, an attempt to order society in light of state service [123]. The high nobility played a dominant role in the reign of Peter's grandson, Peter II (1727–30), and the extensive changes in Russian local administration decreed by Catherine II (1762–96), especially the reorganisation of provincial government and justice in 1775, have been attributed to a desire to enlist the cooperation of the nobility. The Charter of the Nobility (1785) increased noble privileges [120, 122].

The Glorious Revolution was followed by major constitutional changes, including the establishment of regular parliamentary elections by the Triennial Act of 1694, and institutional developments, such as the foundation of the Bank of England in 1694. In combination they led to a significant transformation in the power of the British state. The constitutional changes brought a sense of accountability. Though monarchs and their ministers could hope to employ government patronage to create a reliable parliamentary majority, their control over Parliament was not secure. Government policies were scrutinised carefully and many parliamentarians prized their independence, while the need to consider their electorate, however small, affected many MPs. The parliamentary problems of William III in 1698–1701 forced him to abandon his ministers and lessened his international credibility in a sensitive diplomatic situation, while in the 1733 'Excise Crisis' the apparently secure ministry of Sir Robert Walpole was forced to withdraw a major piece of financial legislation. The need to win parliamentary support encouraged monarchs and ministers to adopt policies that appeared acceptable, while monarchs needed at least one senior minister who had the confidence of the House of Commons, the body that voted parliamentary taxation. Local government was left largely to the Justices of the Peace, commissions of the local gentry. Though the new political system might appear unstable, with frequent changes of ministry, especially in 1689–1724, 1754–70 and 1782–3, in fact it represented and sustained a redefinition of crown–elite relations that was based on cooperation, albeit one tempered by Jacobite disaffection until 1746 and with few links with the Catholic majority of the Irish population. A consequence of this was stronger government finances, as parliamentary support underwrote the development of a stable funded national debt. This served to sustain Britain through a number of expensive wars in which she not only financed her own worldwide military efforts, but also subsidised allies, such as Austria in the wars of the Spanish and Austrian Succession, and Prussia in the Seven Years War, and paid other rulers, such as the Landgraves of Hesse-Cassel and, more controversially, the king as Elector of Hanover, to provide troops for service with the British army. Thanks to parliamentary finance, Britain was able to fund an expansion in her military effort. The average annual size of the army and navy during the Nine Years War was 117,000; during the War of American Independence it was 190,000 [112, 113].

*Nobles and armies*

It was the position of the nobility that was central to the crucial European military change between 1660 and 1760, the growth in the size of armies. The officer corps of these larger forces were dominated by them, the notion of service increasingly acceptable as a result of the opportunities opened by royal favour in the new armies. The social privileges of officers were translated into military life. There were 38 officers' servants and batmen in the Earl of Loudoun's regiment in 1748. The dominance of noble officers ensured that armies were not generally viewed as alien forces, intrusions on local society of an autocratic monarch, and this aided recruiting, not least in the conscription and militia systems that spread in this period. These systems were dependent on the cooperation of the local elites and in them the social relationships of landowner and peasant were often repeated exactly, the same men being officers and soldiers respectively, although the extent to which armies reproduced relationships between nobles and peasants is unclear.

Many nobles had only a limited interest in military activities. In Italy and Spain there was a lack of enthusiasm for military service. The British elite was not a conspicuously military group, though martial traditions and a relative shortage of acceptable profitable local activities helped to make the Scots important in this respect, a course that their Catholicism denied to the Irish unless they wished to serve in foreign armies, as many did, especially in that of France. Nevertheless, war led to an increase in military enthusiasm in Britain. In 1759, during the Seven Years War, Thomas Dampier, Lower Master at Eton, noted: 'There is such a military spirit in the young gentry of the nation at present.' Two years earlier the third Duke of Richmond, a lieutenant colonel though only 22, wrote to his younger brother Lord George Lennox who was eventually to become a general, complaining of his own inexperience and claiming that he was unsuitable for any post of responsibility: 'Persons of rank should be prefer'd young and out of their turns. Everybody says so, but why, because they are the persons to whom the nation should choose to entrust their safety in giving them command as having so much property.' He was to rise to be Master General of the Ordnance and a field marshal. The views of the elite were heeded in military matters. The Earl of Sandwich wrote to an unnamed senior minister in about 1760, seeking the removal of troops from Huntingdon, a borough where he had great influence, and put him in mind 'of what he said in the beginning of the sessions of the house, that no Member of Parliament had ever applied to him to remove the troops from any place where they were complained of, but that he had complied with his request'.

The military origins and traditions of the nobility were generally accepted and regarded as an essential aspect of their distinctiveness and claim to special privileges, especially in eastern Europe. If many nobles did not become officers, most officers were nobles by birth and many of those who were not became so by creation. Commoners were best represented in the artillery and among the engineers. Military service was prestigious and was rewarded with honours, aristocratic promotion, and other benefits. All of the five generals promoted as Knights of the Golden Fleece in Vienna in 1753 were aristocrats. The reverse side of the relationship was that officers often had to use their personal wealth to pay recruiting bounties and to secure vital supplies for their men. Their ability to do so further encouraged their appointment and the purchase of boots or uniforms for their men symbolised the dynamic fusion of crown and elite interests in the states and armies of the period. Many regiments were named after their colonels.

In seventeenth-century France the crown faced the problem of funding a larger military establishment and responded to it by putting pressure on officers to bear a large part of the costs both of raising troops and maintaining them in the field. In return for raising units, commonly from their estates or through their provincial contacts, officers were usually permitted to appoint their subordinate officers. The correspondence and memoirs of the nobility were full of complaints about the major personal expense involved in military service and numerous petitions were presented on behalf of officers who claimed to have ruined themselves in royal service. The willingness of nobles to finance military activity was a reflection of the role that military service still enjoyed in confirming or asserting noble status. As a result of the continuing social prestige attached to military service, the demand for military posts commonly exceeded the supply. In consequence it was generally less expensive for the crown to authorise the raising of a fresh unit, rather than paying to maintain existing ones that had lost much of their strength, because the cost would generally be borne by the new commander. This threatened the continuation of experienced units since their commanders, faced with inadequate government support, were obliged to draw on their own resources.

However, dependence on the financial role of noble officers made it difficult to discipline them. Officers resorted to fraud in order to reduce their costs while large numbers would be absent from their units at any one time. When Louis XIV reduced the size of the army after peace was negotiated with Spain in 1659, while maintaining wartime levels of taxation, the revenue was used to support a standing army of about 60,000 whose costs were substantially met by the government. In return standards of discipline and control were imposed, but this policy was essentially abandoned as the pressure to field larger armies during Louis' wars obliged the government to resort to many of the expedients that had flourished during the 1635–59 war with Spain, including a reliance on the financial contributions of the officers. Their indiscipline, absenteeism and corruption became serious problems again and ministerial control of the army slackened.

The French crown remained dependent upon the personal resources and connections of its officers, which helped to ensure continuity in the dominance of the nobility throughout the officer-corps. French officers paid most of the enlistment bounties in the 1720s and in the Seven Years War often provided the pay of their soldiers themselves. Elsewhere there was a similar dominance. In Austria the new seventeenth-century tendency of aristocratic dynasties to adopt inheritance practices that generally led to single heirs increased the problem of providing for cadets, many of whom flocked into the army. Frederick II was not keen on non-noble officers so that in the Prussian army of 1786 only one-tenth of the officers were commoners, and the proportion among senior ranks was even smaller. Rapid promotion within the French army reflected wealth, but most of the wealthiest officers were from the traditional aristocracy. An aristocratic reaction has been discerned in the French army under Louis XVI, in which the purchase of commissions, a process condemned by poor nobles as benefiting wealthy commoners, was limited after

1776, but as opportunities for advancement by commoners had always been limited, the concept of a reaction is probably overstated. The decision to make all new appointments as sub-lieutenants subject to competitive examinations was not taken in France until the National Assembly passed a decree in 1790. The principal beneficiaries of Louis XVI's bounty among the troops who served in America during the War of American Independence were the comparatively young members of the court aristocracy who already enjoyed a rank disproportionate to their age and experience. In contrast the poor nobles who made up the lower and middle officer grades received fewer marks of favour and many were dissatisfied. Only a dozen non-commissioned officers were promoted from the ranks during the campaign. The French navy was even more socially exclusive as naval commissions were not sold, and social influence played a major role in appointments.

The purchase system for British army commissions helped to restrict promotion from the ranks. Sir James Lowther MP noted in 1742: 'Hardly any rise much in the Army without buying most part of the advances they make, and at the same time selling what they had before. This is the common way except after hot services and being in such climates as the West Indies where many are carried off' (Cumbria Record Office D/Lons/W). Two years later Marshal Wade was confident that the purchase system was providing able officers. He noted that each new officer: 'had the liberty of course to dispose of his own commission to enable him to make up the consideration he was to give to the invalid who quitted.... I have filled the regiment with useful officers' (Bodleian Library MS Eng. Hist. c. 314). In Austria, however, the system of proprietorship of regiments was limited under Maria Theresa and Joseph II by a renewed stress on recognising and rewarding merit that led to the promotion of talented but poorly connected foreigners such as the Baltic German Ernst Laudon (Loudon) and the Anglo-Irish Francis Lacy. In Britain George I and George II limited property rights so that, 'by 1766, executive control over the semi-autonomous regimental concerns had been greatly extended and a transformation wrought on the venal character of officership' [66].

The proportion of the nobility who participated in military life varied. It was greater in eastern than western Europe, with the important exception of the large and generally impoverished Polish nobility who, if they sought military employment, largely did so in private forces or abroad. In most of eastern Europe, military employment opportunities were greater and alternatives fewer, there were stronger traditions of state service, especially in the army, among the nobility, and the poverty of large sections of the rural economy encouraged military service. It is in these areas that conscription systems to provide soldiers developed most fully and where it is most appropriate to discern a militarised society [139]. The very contrasting development of Prussia and Poland suggests that it is inappropriate to regard the socio-economic structure of eastern Europe, with its weak peasantry and important production of goods, especially grain, for western Europe, as in some way leading to a particular political system. Much about the nature of social relations and government on the local level is still unclear, but it is apparent that cooperation between rulers and nobilities was crucial. When Peter I conquered the Baltic provinces from Sweden he took care to respect most of their privileges and their nobility came to play a major role in Russia. As in all periods and countries, it is easy to detect signs of division and conflict in the European states between 1660 and 1760, but the extent of cooperation is impressive, and it would be wrong to regard disputes as in some fashion incompatible with stability or as signs of incipient political breakdown.

## (ii) A militarised society?

Military preparedness could lead to success in conflict and the demands created by this preparedness, and by war itself, constituted the principal burden of government activity. These demands pressed differently upon the people of Europe, varying chronologically, nationally and socially, but they became more pressing from the late seventeenth century as effective conscription and militia systems replaced in part the use of paid volunteers and as the size and cost of armed forces rose.

The ability to strike first and hard, as France did against the Dutch in 1672, and against Austria in 1733 and 1741, and as Prussia did against Austria in 1740, produced obvious benefits for rulers who retained a large peacetime army. Their actions were watched with concern by other powers and only they enjoyed a real freedom of manoeuvre in international relations. As a result there was considerable pressure in certain states to increase the level of military preparedness, an expensive business. This was particularly true of Austria, Prussia and Russia. Their military competitiveness ensured that their combined military preponderance in Europe increased from 1700 and especially 1740, just as that of Austria and France on land, and of England, France and the United Provinces at sea had increased from the 1660s and the mid-seventeenth century respectively with obvious political consequences. Bavaria and Sardinia cited vulnerability to Austrian attack as their reason for rejecting Anglo-French alliance proposals in 1726. Frederick II noted one result of the Austrian military reforms after the War of the Austrian Succession, when he commented in 1749 that Maria Theresa was trying to obtain from each province in peacetime what they had paid in war. However, even the states with the largest forces increased their armies in wartime: Louis XIV for each of his wars, Frederick II during the First and Second Silesian Wars, Catherine II (the Great) of Russia during her war with Turkey in 1768–74, or Joseph II of Austria in 1787 in preparation for attacking Turkey [140].

The armies retained by weaker powers did not compare with those of the major states, one of the significant military and political developments of the post-1660 period being their increasing discrepancy. The army of Moldavia in 1700 was less than 8,000, scarcely able to compete with that of Turkey. Mazepa's army in the Ukraine in 1700 was about 40,000, that of Russia considerably more and the Ukraine was easily overrun in 1708, the Zaporozhian Cossacks being crushed by the Russians the following year. The growth of the Austrian and Prussian armies was not matched by that of the other German states [138], both cause and effect of their weakness. The forces of the Electorate of Cologne and Prince-Bishopric of Münster rose from about 22,000 in 1728 to 25,000 in 1762.

In 1745 the army of the Elector of Mainz was 7,500 strong; in the 1770s the impoverished Landgrave of Hesse Darmstadt could afford only 5,000 troops, whom he enjoyed drilling, while in 1785 the Prince-Bishop of Würzburg controlled three battalions of infantry and one regiment of dragoons, the latter without the extra cost of actual horses. In 1761 the French foreign minister Choiseul pressed a Saxon agent on the need for Augustus III not to neglect his army as he had done in the past and to use the forthcoming peace in order to re-establish a force which could make Saxony respected by her neighbours, by whom Choiseul meant Prussia. He added that such an army would enable Augustus to preserve and increase his possessions. The agent replied by stressing the need for money.

Many of the small forces were never used militarily and were too small to produce a field army capable of fighting a battle effectively, but their existence is a reminder of the extent to which Europe was imbued with military concerns. Armies were generally seen as an essential attribute of sovereignty, while, as the largest force of men at the disposal of rulers, they were often used for unwarlike purposes. The general absence of national police forces increased this tendency, as did the fact that most forces were small and under local control. Troops were therefore used for many policing purposes, especially in rural and frontier areas where police forces were generally weak and the task of maintaining order difficult, even without attempting the harder problem of enforcing laws on a systematic basis. The violence involved in some policing, and the size of possible problems, encouraged the use of troops. They were used against smugglers, often being the only effective government presence in frontier regions. The French used troops against smugglers in Dauphiné in the early 1730s and on Belle Ile in 1764. They were also used against bandits, against whom police forces were often ineffective. In 1779, 1,000 Neapolitan troops were sent to attack the bandits of Calabria, an area where government authority was very weak. Troops were used against rioters, as in Glasgow in 1725, Newcastle in 1740 and France in 1768 and 1770, and in industrial disputes, French soldiers intervening against the Sedan clothworkers in 1750. Though the

French army was increasingly located on the frontiers and used less for police duties, it did not altogether lose this role, being used to enforce the cordon created around Marseilles during the 1720 outbreak of plague. Elsewhere police functions remained important and sometimes, as in Russia, increased. The Russian army administered and collected taxes, especially the poll tax introduced by Peter I in 1718, carried out censuses and acted as a police force.

The danger of rebellions across much of Europe ensured that military forces had to be prepared to confront them, a task made easier by their limited regard for peasants and by their discipline. French troops suppressed revolts in the Boulogne region in 1662, the Vivarais in 1670, Bordeaux and Brittany in 1675, more effectively than the forces used against the Croquants in 1636 and the Va-Nu-Pieds in 1639. In 1751 Austrian troops had to be used in Croatia to suppress a rising inspired by the fear of a loss of regional privileges. The Pugachev revolt of 1773–4, a peasant-Cossack rising in Russia, led to pitched battles such as Tatishchevo in 1774.

Troops could also be used for purposes that bore little relation to policing activities. Just as officers in the Prussian cantonal conscription system used troops for work on their estates, so rulers employed them as a labour force, both for military purposes – as with the soldiers used to construct roads and forts to control the Scottish Highlands after the suppression of the Jacobite risings in 1715 and 1745, and the 16,000 soldiers used as workmen on Bohemian fortifications in 1786 – and for other tasks, such as canal construction by Peter I. Armies could be utilised for social purposes. The Bavarian minister Count Rumford was keen to use the army in the 1780s to introduce useful improvements. He established military gardens, with the intention of publicising new agricultural methods and crops, particularly the potato, and regimental schools that would also educate the children of the local peasantry. The non-military use of troops could lead to conflict with civilians, as when garrison labour was employed to weave or to repair shoes. In some cases, as with harvesting, it could lead to a conflict between military and civilian purposes.

Armies served functional purposes, but they were also of

value for their part in enabling rulers and, to a lesser extent, aristocrats to fulfil the role attributed to them and which they were generally willing to discharge. Military leadership was an important role, one sanctioned by history, dynastic tradition and biblical example. In 1788 the Austrian Chancellor, Prince Kaunitz, tried to oppose this. Urging Joseph II to abandon the personal command of his armies against the Turks in the Balkans, he drew attention to examples of rulers, past and present, who left such command to their generals, 'in order to concentrate on what is properly the job of the ruler, the government and general surveillance of the state they have received from Providence'. Some rulers displayed little interest in war or military affairs. Ferdinand VI of Spain (1746–59) concentrated on domestic matters and stayed neutral in the Seven Years War, despite the arguments of his French ally that British successes in North America were destroying the colonial balance of power. Denmark was at peace from 1720 for the rest of the century, with the exception of a very brief attack on Sweden in 1788. Military reviews were still important for the Danish court. Many rulers saw war as their function and justification as defenders of their subjects and inheritance, a source of personal glory, dynastic aggrandisement and national fortune. Some central and eastern European rulers served in person, such as Charles XII [52], Peter I or Frederick William of Brandenburg-Prussia, who led his troops in Alsace in 1674–5, his eldest son dying of an epidemic there in December 1674. Frederick IV of Denmark and Frederick William I of Prussia accompanied the attack on the Swedish-held island of Rügen in 1715. But they were not alone: Louis XIV went on a number of campaigns, such as the attacks on the United Provinces in 1672 and on Franche-Comté in 1674. William III beat James II at the battle of the Boyne in 1690 and fought the French at Steenkerk (1692) and Neerwinden (1693). Victor Amadeus of Savoy-Piedmont led his troops in a number of battles including Staffarda (1690) and Turin (1706) [136]. George II was at Dettingen (1743), Louis XV at Fontenoy (1745). The only significant exceptions were female rulers, though they also could benefit by association with victory, as did Anne of Britain and Anna, Elizabeth and Catherine II of Russia.

Victories against the Turks in the war of 1768–74 gave Catherine the prestige to compensate for the questionable circumstances of her accession. Emulation of ancestors, former monarchs and contemporaries played a role in the desire to fight. Louis XIV compared himself with his grandfather, Henry IV. In 1741 the French scientist Maupertuis commented: 'after having studied very closely the character of the King of Prussia, that that Prince's great misfortune is to have heard that there had been a Charles XII of Sweden in the world'.

Frederick II's dedication to military success was no greater than that of Charles XII, or Peter I, who led his forces as far from Russia as the southern shores of the Caspian and Copenhagen, where in 1716 he saw the ovens constructed to cook bread for the troops before going to the palace. Nonetheless, Frederick's successful combination of political and military leadership made a great impression. He led his army throughout his reign, drilling it and conducting major manoeuvres in peace and winning a series of spectacular victories in war. Kaunitz admitted that Frederick's example proved an exception to the rule he sought to lay down to Joseph II, who wished to win a comparable military reputation. Frederick's approach to war was certainly not a casual one, of war as a courtly activity, a royal sport, a variation on hunting, as it had appeared in some of the literature of the sixteenth century. The chivalric notion of personal honour and exemplary reputation that had led commanders to place themselves in the van had been replaced by prudent generalship so that the wounding of a royal general, like Charles XII at Poltava (1709), was now exceptional. Frederick saw war as a duty to be best discharged through training and dedication, an attitude that he sought to disseminate in Prussia. His poem the *Art of War*, written in 1749, revealed his belief in the need for detailed planning and cautious execution. It was reinforced in detailed confidential works of instruction written for his officers [56].

The military role of monarchs was not therefore confined to war. It encompassed peacetime supervision of the army, a role that provided rulers with excitement, a sense of mission and an opportunity to display themselves in a favourable light as leaders. When George I reviewed his footguards in Hyde Park in July 1724 he was accompanied by his senior ministers, several ambassadors and many of the nobility. The previous year a Secretary of State accompanying George to Hanover wrote of, 'the government of the army, which he would never bear to be controlled in, neither in his country nor in England'. Military supervision involved a considerable amount of time for most rulers, whether it was Charles Emmanuel III of Sardinia going with two sons in 1757 to inspect fortifications, or George III gaining popularity and displaying British power in 1773 by visiting the fleet. Ferdinand IV of Naples was keen on military exercises, with a definite taste and talent for army manoeuvres, and spent much time on them. Having reviewed the Maltese fleet in July 1776, he took part in a simulated naval conflict the following month. The army helped in the display of power and in February 1777 Ferdinand manoeuvred his troops for the benefit of the visiting Frederick II of Hesse-Cassel, who had led the Hessian contingent sent to oppose the Jacobites in Scotland in 1746. Having spent the spring of 1777 training his corps of marine cadets Ferdinand took part in a campaign with them in the summer, involving mock battles and sieges and a plan of campaign drawn up by himself. Ferdinand's interest was in no way exceptional, though few other monarchs would have made three surprise visits to troop quarters in a month, as he did in 1778, finding poor discipline, quarters and fortifications. As success and prestige were both enjoyable and the lubricant of obedience, it was understandable that many monarchs sought them through military activities. Several of the so-called Enlightened Despots, the monarchs of the later eighteenth century, were military men, for example Frederick II.

A definite trend towards the wearing of military uniform at court can be discerned. In 1723 a British official visiting Berlin found that 'choice soldiers well armed and well trained' were Frederick William I's 'reigning passion' and noted that everyone wore uniform, adding 'to strangers it is very odd at first'. Officers of the French and Austrian armies were often reluctant to wear uniforms in the first half of the century. However, after 1763 Joseph II and his successors always wore uniform at court and on formal occasions. Joseph changed into his field marshal's uniform when dying. This trend was resisted only at the courts of Madrid and Versailles. Military uniform was the clothing of order and obedient hierarchy; it encapsulated the participation of nobles in the service state, the systematisation of the personal links binding nobilities and monarchs.

The identification of states with military activities could create a sense of patriotism, a civic or secular counterpart of religious loyalties. Local privileges were, however, vigorously protected against military infringement, particularly if they prohibited or limited recruitment, billeting and providing other resources for the armed forces. This could lead to tension. In 1697 an English Secretary of State reported:

> The Mayor of Portsmouth with some of his brethren attended the Council yesterday upon a complaint from the dockyard that the town had violently broke down their gates and rid through in triumph. On the other side they said it was no more than their ordinary procession of going the bounds of their parish as is everywhere practised on Holy Thursday and that the officers of the yards shut their gates against them contrary to all former usage. Both sides were found in blame one for denying entrance and the other for forcing it and they were directed to live more friendly together for the future.

Pacifist sentiment was not widely expressed. The intellectuals and religious figures who condemned aggressive war, such as the French *philosophes*, appear to have enjoyed little support. There was little sense that *ancien régime* society could exist without war. In the United Provinces in the 1780s the Patriots, a movement of the middling orders against the house of Orange, criticised attempts to expand the army as a needless and dangerous extravagance. However, the condemnation of a standing army that formed such an important part of Opposition rhetoric in Britain in the seventeenth and eighteenth centuries found little echo on the continent. This condemnation in any case was political, not pacifist, in its stance, as could be seen in Opposition pressure for the creation of a strong militia, which led to the Militia Act of 1757 [157].

Republics and limited monarchies tended to have small armies. The customary peacetime establishment of the British army was 18,000 in the late 1720s, 26,000 in the 1730s and 29,000 in the early 1750s, excluding the force, generally of 12,000, paid for out of Irish revenues. This force, which was supplemented in wartime, was inadequate for British purposes. When troops had to be sent abroad, or preparations made to resist invasion or rebellion, as in 1715, 1745 and 1756, it was necessary to seek Dutch or German military assistance. Poland, an elective monarchy with a very weak central government, had a tiny army, its size fixed at 24,000 by the Diet in 1717, which made no adequate provisions for its support. Attempts at the Diet of 1718 to increase the size of the army and to finance the artillery and upkeep of fortresses were unsuccessful. Political strife prevented any further reform until the 1760s and the small force was poorly trained and usually under strength. This did not, however, reflect an anti-military ethos as the private armies, such as that of Count Stanislaus Radziwill, equalled them in training. In Sweden the death of Charles XII, killed in 1718 while invading Norway, had been followed by constitutional changes limiting royal authority and creating the so-called Age of Liberty (1719–72). The mid-century Swedish army was weak, below strength, poorly led and administered and handicapped by a highly politicised, divided officer corps. The fleet was also weak with only three ships launched between 1756 and 1772 and only eight fit for service in 1769 [153]. However, the size and quality of the British navy or of the Swiss troops in foreign service suggest that it would be foolish to regard the small armies of such states as evidence of any disinclination to fight. The enthusiasm with which Britain attacked Spain in 1739 [140: 185–209] and Sweden Russia two years later [141: 78] indicates that powerful and well-armed rulers were not the sole instigators of war.

By adopting a different chronology of military development and proposing a definition of absolutism in terms of elite consensus, a new causal relationship between military development and political change can be offered. The origins of late-seventeenth-century absolutism can be found both in the long-term search for a restatement of order in reaction to the turmoil of the sixteenth century, a period of acute disorder that had political, social and religious dimensions, and in a series of political crises in the first half of the seventeenth. The most important of these were not the troubles of the 1640s and, to a lesser extent, the 1650s that are usually described in terms of a mid-seventeenth-century crisis, but the reimposition of an effective Catholic hegemony in France and the dominions of the Austrian Habsburgs in the 1620s. This did not automatically lead to civil order and good crown–elite relations, as the *Fronde* demonstrates, but it created the necessary coherent ideological and political context within which such relations could develop and be encouraged, not least by traditional methods of patronage.

# Conclusion

This work has sought to show the relationship between the sixteenth and seventeenth centuries on the one hand and the eighteenth on the other, periods all too often studied in isolation, and in particular to argue that it is unhelpful to place too much weight on a mid-seventeenth-century division. The notion of a military revolution in the early modern period has been challenged and it has been argued that the changes commonly stressed in the period 1560–1660 can be qualified both by considering the claims that have been advanced and by ranging more widely to consider the situation throughout Europe. A concentration on warfare in the last decades of the period suggests that the notion of a revolution is inappropriate. In so far as a military revolution occurred in the early modern period it could be dated more appropriately to the hundred years, especially the first fifty, after the period highlighted by Roberts. This is equally the case whether attention is devoted to weaponry and tactics, where the introduction of the bayonet and the phasing-out of the pike were of considerable importance, or to the position in a number of crucial states – France, Austria, Russia, Prussia and Britain – which emerged as the European great powers in this period and retained that position until 1918 [141, 149]. The military changes of the period 1660–1760 were considerable and they included a dramatic growth in the firepower of the major naval powers and an important increase in the firepower and trained manpower available in the major armies. However, the technological changes that were to bring military superiority for the European powers in Africa and Asia did not occur until the following century [78].

Two major reasons for offering different conclusions to those of Roberts and Parker have been advanced. The first is a re-examination of the period 1560–1660 and, specifically, of the Thirty Years War. This suggests that Roberts' explanation of Swedish success as being in large part due to tactical innovations is unfounded. Instead, stress has been placed on size of armies, morale and tactical flexibility. The second is a consideration of the hundred years after 1660, a period neglected by Roberts and, more seriously, by Parker, the title of whose book suggests misleadingly that he covered it. The qualitative and quantitative changes in warfare in this period, especially in terms of infantry tactics and the size of the armed forces of the major powers, throw a new light on the limited nature of the changes in 1560–1660. Indeed, the significance of those years had been downplayed by Parker's stress on the implications of improvements in artillery in the fifteenth century and the development of the *trace italienne*, which directed his attention to the late-fifteenth and early-sixteenth centuries, offering a largely understated corrective to Roberts' thesis. Parker sought to accommodate his own chronological perspective to that of Roberts, just as he had earlier reconciled his own work on the Spanish army with that of Roberts on Dutch and Swedish developments. The essential differences between their accounts have been largely ignored.

Possibly it is best to put aside the provocative, but ultimately unconvincing, thesis of Roberts and, instead, to suggest that innovation and development were concentrated in the late fifteenth and then again in the late seventeenth centuries. Whatever chronology is devised, it is necessary to accept both that not all areas moved at the same pace and that their failure to do so was not necessarily the consequence of an inability to develop at the proper pace, as if some model of universal applicability existed. Far more research is required on developments in eastern Europe, but also too little is known about the armed forces of western Europe. This is especially true of the Portuguese army, of the post-1660 Spanish army, of the armed forces of most Italian states in the seventeenth and eighteenth centuries and of those of many German rulers. In addition, a hard look at the reality of activity behind claims of military strength, such as has been offered brilliantly by David Parrott in his work on the French army under Richelieu, might well yield fresh insights and undermine widely held views that are in fact based on limited or slanted archival evidence. There is also need for a re-examination of many campaigns and conflicts. The War of the Austrian Succession has received insufficient attention.

The impact of war and military activity on early modern Europe is not easy to assess. Specific effects can be measured: taxes and recruitment produced extensive paperwork. Particular groups benefited, such as the Northampton shoemakers ordered to make 2,000 pairs of shoes for the British army in 1746 or the Styrian peasants who were given contracts shortly afterwards to supply the Austrian army with artillery horses. However, the intangible effects of military activity, in terms of the role of the army as a model for social organisation and the relationship between government and military development, are harder to gauge. The situation clearly varied chronologically and nationally. In terms of direction and inspiration from the top, rulers differed in their policies. The nature of the external threat varied as did the extent of domestic resources, and yet both of these could be crucial in creating the necessities and opportunities that affected decisions on matters such as recruitment policy. In adopting a long-term and continent-wide perspective and having only a brief space in which to employ it there is a danger that variations will be elided. Certainly the process of consensus and cooperation that I would argue was crucial to the development of a domestic context enabling military growth was not without its difficulties and setbacks. Yet it is appropriate to see this process as the complement of international competition, rather than to argue that the latter led to any supposed politico-administrative revolution producing centralised, bureaucratic and autocratic states able to coerce society and direct it to produce the means of destruction. *Leviathan* (1651) was the title of a work of speculative thought, the theoretical creation of Thomas Hobbes, not a description of early modern European government.

The relationship between international conflict and military development is a difficult problem. It is possible to point to specific periods of activity in response to particular crises; for example, Austrian reforms after the War of the Austrian Succession. More research is required on this subject, in assessing, for example, how far the major change in infantry weaponry in 1680–1710 – the replacement of matchlocks and pikes by flintlocks with socket bayonets – and the pace of the change arose from problems encountered in the fighting of these years, from theoretical reflections and from emulation. It would also be useful to ascertain the extent to which these changes were affected by the industrial capacity of different countries.

War is often seen as a forcer of innovation, technical in the form of new weaponry, governmental and social in the shape of the demands created by the burdens of major conflicts. This argument should not be pushed too far when considering early modern European society. The expanded armed forces of the period developed in a fashion that did not challenge the social reality of societies organised around the principles of inegalitarianism and inheritance. Larger armies brought more opportunities to nobles, who benefited both from the assumption that they were naturally suited for positions of command and from the fact that in general this was the case. Thus, the armies were not forces 'outside' society, but rather reflections of patterns of social control and influence and the beliefs that gave cohesion to these patterns.

This situation was challenged in the late eighteenth century. British officers in the War of American Independence were surprised by the modest social status of some of the rebel officers. A military ethos centred on the ideal of patriotic volunteer units played a major role in that conflict, the French Revolutionary Wars and during the last years of independent Poland in the early 1790s. The Act of Confederation issued in Cracow in March 1794 called 'all citizens' to arms. Polish peasants were encouraged to volunteer with the prospect of freedom from serfdom. In practice, most of the officers in these forces were men of property, but the developments of the last decades of the century suggested that armies could serve to overthrow established social and political lineaments rather than to reflect and strengthen them. This toppling of much of the *ancien régime* was achieved by the armies of revolutionary France and in so doing they were certainly revolutionary. The revolutionary ethos and purposes of the French army in the 1790s transformed the political context of military activity.

# Select Bibliography

There is space to list only a few works and, for the benefit of the student, only works in English are cited, while recent books have been emphasised. Periodical literature and earlier works can best be approached through the bibliographies and footnotes of these books. The notes in [4] are especially useful.

### Theory of the military revolution

[1] M. Roberts, *The Military Revolution, 1560–1660* (1956), reprinted in Roberts (ed.), *Essays in Swedish History* (1967). The original, concise statement of the thesis.

[2] M. D. Feld, 'Middle-class society and the rise of military professionalism. The Dutch Army 1559–1609', *Armed Forces and Society* (1975).

[3] G. Parker, 'The Military Revolution, 1560–1660 – a myth?', *Journal of Modern History* (1976), reprinted in Parker, *Spain and the Netherlands 1559–1659* (1979). Modifies, without rejecting, Roberts.

[4] ——, *The Military Revolution. Military Innovation and the Rise of the West, 1500–1800* (1988). Valuable reflective work, strong on naval and trans-oceanic warfare, weak on eighteenth century. Important critical review by J. Plowright, *British Army Review*, 90 (Dec. 1988).

[5] R. Porter and M. Teich (eds), *Revolution in History* (1986). Valuable on idea of revolution, but fails to consider warfare.

### 1560–1660 reassessed

[6] G. N. Clark, *War and Society in the Seventeenth Century* (1958). A valuable survey that popularised the idea of military revolution.

[7] P. Contamine, *War in the Middle Ages* (1984). A classic.

[8] A. Corvisier, *Armies and Societies in Europe, 1494–1789* (1979). Disappointing but clear survey.

[9] C. Cruickshank, *Elizabeth's Army* (1966). Valuable study.

[10] C. Duffy, *Siege Warfare: the Fortress in the Early Modern World, 1494–1660* (1979). Best study of the subject.

[11] C. Falls, *Elizabeth's Irish Wars* (1970).

[12] J. R. Hale, *Renaissance War Studies* (1983).

[13] J. R. Hale, *War and Society in Renaissance Europe 1450–1620* (1985). A valuable and wide-ranging study.

[14] —— and M. E. Mallett, *The Military Organization of a Renaissance State: Venice c.1400 to 1617* (1984).

[15] R. Hutton, *The Royalist War Effort 1642–1646* (1982).

[16] H. A. Lloyd, *The Rouen Campaign, 1590–1592* (1973). English intervention in the French Wars of Religion.

[17] J. A. Lynn, 'Tactical Evolution in the French Army 1560–1660', *French Historical Studies* (1985).

[18] ——, 'The Growth of the French Army during the Seventeenth Century', *Armed Forces and Society* (1983). Needs to be read in light of Parrott's work.

[19] W. Majewski, 'The Polish Art of War in the Sixteenth and Seventeenth Centuries', in J. K. Fedorowicz (ed.), *A Republic of Nobles* (1982). The best introduction to Polish warfare.

[20] W. S. Maltby, *Alba* (1983). Philip II's leading general.

[21] G. Parker, *The Army of Flanders and the Spanish Road: the Logistics of Spanish Victory and Defeat 1567–1659* (1972). The major study of the Spanish war machine. See also C. Martin and G. Parker, *The Spanish Armada* (1988).

[22] ——, *The Thirty Years War* (1984). Best work on the subject.

[23] D. A. Parrott, 'Strategy and Tactics in the Thirty Years War: the "Military Revolution"'. *Militärgeschichtliche Mitteilungen* (1985). A valuable corrective based on considerable knowledge.

[24] ——, *The Administration of the French Army during the Ministry of Cardinal Richelieu* (Oxford D.Phil., 1985). A fundamental work of revisionism.

[25] J. V. Polisensky, *The Thirty Years War* (1971). Informed Marxist account.

[26] M. Roberts, *Gustavus Adolphus* (1953–8). Best biography.

[27] R. A. Stradling, *Europe and the Decline of Spain. A Study of the Spanish System, 1580–1720* (1981). Clear and intelligent account.

**Change 1660–1760**

[28] A. Aberg, 'The Swedish Army from Lützen to Narva', in M. Roberts (ed.), *Sweden's Age of Greatness* (1973).

[29] M. S. Anderson, *War and Society in Europe of the Old Regime, 1618–1789* (1988). Judicious overview.

[30] A. Balisch, 'Infantry Battlefield Tactics in the Seventeenth and Eighteenth Centuries on the European and Turkish Theatres of War', *Studies in History and Politics* (1983–4). On Austria.

[31] T. M. Barker, *Double Eagle and Crescent: Vienna's Second Turkish Siege* (1967). 1683.

[32] ——, *The Military Intellectual and Battle: Raimondo Montecuccoli* (1975). Valuable guide to military thought. See also A. Gat, 'Montecuccoli: Humanist Philosophy, Paracelsian Science and Military Theory', *War and Society* (1988).

[33]  D. A. Baugh, *British Naval Administration in the Age of Walpole* (1965). Reveals sophistication of subject.

[34]  J. Black, *Culloden and the '45* (1990). Firepower eventually defeats Jacobitism.

[35]  —— and P. L. Woodfine (eds), *The Royal Navy and the Use of Naval Power in the Eighteenth Century* (1988). One of the most impressive military achievements of the period.

[36]  R. Butler, *Choiseul* (1980). Includes good accounts of French campaigning in the War of the Austrian Succession.

[37]  D. Chandler, *Marlborough as Military Commander* (1973). Excellent on War of the Spanish Succession. See also his *The Art of War in the Age of Marlborough* (1976).

[38]  J. Childs, *The Army of Charles II* (1976). Valuable study of administration.

[39]  ——, *Armies and Warfare in Europe, 1648–1789* (1982). Interesting and wide-ranging.

[40]  ——, *The Army, James II and the Glorious Revolution* (1980). Important discussion of military dimensions of 1688.

[41]  ——, *The British Army of William III, 1689–1702* (1987). Concentrates on administration.

[42]  C. Duffy, *The Wild Goose and the Eagle: a Life of Marshal von Browne, 1705–1757* (1964). Leading Austrian general.

[43]  ——, *The Army of Frederick the Great* (1974). Best writer on eighteenth-century warfare, with a real feel for military life and the period.

[44]  ——, *The Army of Maria Theresa* (1977).

[45]  ——, *Russia's Military Way to the West. Origins and Nature of Russian Military Power 1700–1800* (1981).

[46]  ——, *The Fortress in the Age of Vauban and Frederick the Great* (1985). Scholarly and well-illustrated.

[47]  ——, *Frederick the Great: a Military Life* (1986).

[48]  ——, *The Military Experience in the Age of Reason* (1987).

[49]  M. Duffy (ed.), *The Military Revolution and the State* (1980). Useful essays on British navy and French army.

[50]  J. Ehrman, *The Navy in the War of William III, 1689–1697* (1953).

[51]  A. D. Francis, *The First Peninsular War, 1702–1713* (1975). Iberian aspects of War of the Spanish Succession.

[52]  R. M. Hatton, *Charles XII of Sweden* (1968). Important for Great Northern War.

[53]  R. Hellie, 'The Petrine Army: Continuity, Change and Impact', *Canadian-American Slavic Studies* (1974).

[54]  J. A. Houlding, *Fit for Service. The Training of the British Army 1715–1795* (1981).

[55]  L. Kennett, *The French Armies in the Seven Years War* (1967).

[56]  J. Luvaas, *Frederick the Great on the Art of War* (1966). Frederick's writings.

[57]  B. Menning, 'Russia and the West: The problem of Eighteenth-Century Military Models' in A. Cross (ed.), *Russia and the West in the Eighteenth Century* (1983).

[58] D. McKay, *Prince Eugene of Savoy* (1977).

[59] E. Robson, 'The Armed Forces and the Art of War', in *New Cambridge Modern History*, 7 (1957).

[60] J. M. Stoye, *The Siege of Vienna* (1964). 1683.

[61] C. C. Sturgill, *Marshal Villars and the War of the Spanish Succession* (1965). One of Louis XIV's leading generals.

[62] ———, *Claude Le Blanc* (1975). French Secretary of State for War 1718–23, 1726–8.

[63] J. R. Western, 'War on a New Scale: Professionalism in Armies, Navies and Diplomacy' in A. Cobban (ed.), *The Eighteenth Century* (1969).

## Limitations of change

[64] M. van Creveld, *Supplying War. Logistics from Wallenstein to Patton* (1977). Central role of supply. See also his *Technology and War from 2000 BC to the Present* (1989). On the Turks see C. Finkel, *The Administration of Warfare: the Ottoman Military Campaigns in Hungary, 1593–1606* (1988).

[65] W. Fann, 'Peacetime Attrition in the Army of Frederick William I', *Central European History* (1978). Desertion in the peacetime Prussian army.

[66] A. J. Guy, *Oeconomy and Discipline: Officership and Administration in the British Army 1714–63* (1985).

[67] J. M. Hill, *Celtic Warfare 1595–1763* (1986).

[68] B. P. Hughes, *Firepower Weapons' Effectiveness on the Battlefield 1630–1850* (1974). A fundamental study of an often overlooked subject. See also his *Open Fire: Artillery Tactics from Marlborough to Wellington* (1983).

[69] G. Jewsbury, 'Chaos and Corruption: The Comte de Langeron's Critique of the 1787–1792 Russo-Turkish War', *Studies in History and Politics* (1983–4).

[70] P. Mackesy, *The Coward of Minden* (1979). Breakdown of command structure at a crucial moment.

[71] J. Pritchard, *Louis XV's Navy 1748–1762* (1987). Account of an under-funded service under pressure.

[72] N. A. M. Rodger, *The Wooden World. An Anatomy of the Georgian Navy* (1986). Social study stressing cohesion of marine life.

[73] D. Showalter, 'Tactics and Recruitment in Eighteenth Century Prussia', *Studies in History and Politics* (1983–4).

## Colonial conflict

[74] R. Atwood, *The Hessians. Mercenaries from Hessen-Kassel in the American Revolution* (1980).

[75] C. R. Boxer, *The Dutch Seaborne Empire* (1965).

[76] C. M. Cipolla, *Guns and Sails in the Early Phase of European Expansion 1400–1700* (1965).

[77] M. Duffy, *Soldiers, Sugar and Seapower. The British Expeditions to the West Indies and the War against Revolutionary France* (1987).

[78] D. R. Headrick, *The Tools of Empire: Technology and European Imperialism in the Nineteenth Century* (1981).

[79] D. Higginbotham, *The War of American Independence. Military Attitudes, Policies, and Practice, 1763–1789* (1971).

[80] T. Keppel, *The Life of Augustus Viscount Keppel* (1842).

[81] D. M. Lang, *The Last Years of the Georgian Monarchy 1658–1832* (1957). Russian advance in the Caucasus.

[82] P. Mackesy, *The War for America 1775–1783* (1964). Excellent account from the British point of view.

[83] W. H. McNeill, *Europe's Steppe Frontier 1500–1800* (1964). Turkish advance and retreat.

[84] R. W. Olson, *The Siege of Mosul* (1975). Turkish-Persian conflict in 1730s and 1740s.

[85] P. Paret, 'Colonial Experience and European Military Reform at the end of the Eighteenth Century', *Bulletin of the Institute of Historical Research* (1964).

[86] R. A. Pierce, *Eastward to Empire: Exploration and Conquest on the Russian Open Frontier to 1750* (1973).

[87] K. Roider, *The Reluctant Ally: Austria's Policy in the Austro-Turkish War, 1737–1739* (1972).

[88] P. E. Russell, 'Redcoats in the Wilderness: British Officers and Irregular Warfare in Europe and America, 1740 to 1760', *William and Mary Quarterly* (1978).

[89] S. J. Shaw, *Between Old and New: The Ottoman Empire under Sultan Selim III 1789–1807* (1971).

[90] J. Shy, *A People Numerous and Armed. Reflections on the Military Struggle for American Independence* (1976).

[91] F. and M. Wickwire, *Cornwallis and the War of Independence* (1971). British general defeated in America.

## The coming of revolution

[92] J. P. Bertaud, *The Army of the French Revolution: From Citizen-Soldiers to Instruments of Power* (1988). French authority on the 1790s. See also G. E. Rothenberg, 'Soldiers and the Revolution: the French Army, Society and the State, 1788–99', *Historical Journal* (1989).

[93] G. Best, *War and Society in Revolutionary Europe, 1770–1870* (1982). Judicious survey.

[94] D. Bien, 'The Army in the French Enlightenment: Reform, Reaction and Revolution', *Past and Present* (1979).

[95] J. R. Cobb, *The People's Armies* (1987). Lively study of the radical cutting age of the Revolution. See also A. Forrest, *Conscripts and Deserters. The Army and French Society during the Revolution and Empire* (1989).

[96] J. A. Lynn, *The Bayonets of the Republic. Motivation and Tactics in the Army of Revolutionary France* (1984).

101

[97] P. Paret, 'Napoleon and the Revolution in War' in Paret (ed.), *Makers of Modern Strategy from Machiavelli to the Nuclear Age* (1986). Important for limitations of Napoleonic warfare.

[98] R. Quimby, *The Background of Napoleonic Warfare* (1957).

[99] S. Ross, 'The Development of the Combat Division in Eighteenth-Century French Armies', *French Historical Studies* (1965).

[100] ——, *From Flintlock to Rifle. Infantry Tactics, 1740–1866* (1979).

[101] G. E. Rothenberg, *The Art of Warfare in the Age of Napoleon* (1977). Able survey.

[102] ——, *Napoleon's Great Adversaries: The Archduke Charles and the Austrian Army, 1792–1814* (1982).

[103] S. F. Scott, *The Response of the Royal Army to the French Revolution: The Role and Development of the Line Army during 1789–93* (1978).

[104] D. Stone, 'Patriotism and Professionalism: The Polish Army in the Eighteenth Century', *Studies in History and Politics* (1983–4). Development of army in the last years of independence.

## Absolutism and military change

[105] P. Anderson, *Lineages of the Absolutist State* (1974). Marxist approach.

[106] T. Aston (ed.), *Crisis in Europe, 1560–1660* (1965). Mid-seventeenth-century crisis.

[107] W. Beik, *Absolutism and Society in Seventeenth-Century France* (1985). Detailed study of Languedoc.

[108] D. Bitton, *The French Nobility in Crisis, 1560–1640* (1969).

[109] J. Black, *Europe in the Eighteenth Century, 1700–1789* (1990).

[110] T. C. W. Blanning, *Joseph II and Enlightened Despotism* (1970).

[111] R. J. Bonney, *Political Change in France under Richelieu and Mazarin 1624–1661* (1978).

[112] J. Brewer, *The Sinews of Power. War, Money and the English State, 1688–1783* (1989).

[113] P. Dickson, *The Financial Revolution in England* (1967). Detailed study of change after 1688.

[114] J. H. Elliott, *The Revolt of the Catalans* (1963).

[115] ——, *The Count-Duke of Olivares* (1986). Monumental biography that throws much light on the 'decline' of Spain.

[116] R. J. W. Evans, *The Making of the Habsburg Monarchies 1550–1700* (1979). Brilliant study of creation of absolutist, Catholic ideology.

[117] R. Forster and J. P. Greene (eds), *Preconditions of Revolution in Early Modern Europe* (1970). Comparative approach to major crises.

[118] R. Hatton (ed.), *Louis XIV and Absolutism* (1976).

[119] K. J. V. Jespersen, 'Social Change and Military Revolution in Early Modern Europe: Some Danish Evidence', *Historical Journal* (1983).

[120] R. E. Jones, *The Emancipation of the Russian Nobility, 1762–1785* (1973).

[121] R. E. Jones, *Provincial Development in Russia. Catherine II and Jakob Sievers* (1984). Valuable study of provincial government in practice.

[122] J. P. LeDonne, *Ruling Russia. Politics and Administration in the Age of Absolutism, 1762–1796* (1984).

[123] B. Meehan-Waters, *Autocracy and Aristocracy: the Russian Service Elite of 1730* (1982).

[124] R. Mettam, *Power and Faction in Louis XIV's France* (1988). Important work of revisionism.

[125] D. Parker, *La Rochelle and the French Monarchy: Conflict and Order in Seventeenth-Century France* (1980). Suppression of Huguenot independence.

[126] G. Parker, *Spain and the Netherlands 1559–1659* (1979).

[127] ——— and L. M. Smith (eds), *The General Crisis of the Seventeenth Century* (1978).

[128] C. Peterson, *Peter the Great's Administrative and Judicial reforms* (1979).

[129] T. K. Rabb, *The Struggle for Stability in Early Modern Europe* (1975). General crisis re-examined.

[130] M. Raeff, *The Well-Ordered Police State. Social and Institutional Change through Law in the Germanies and Russia, 1660–1800* (1983). Development of the idea and practice of the state as improver of society through legislation.

[131] M. Roberts, *The Early Vasas: a History of Sweden 1523–1611* (1968).

[132] J. H. M. Salmon, *Society in Crisis: France in the Sixteenth Century* (1975). Excellent account of French Wars of Religion.

[133] J. H. Shennan, *The Origins of the Modern European State, 1450–1725* (1974). Stresses modernity of period.

[134] ———, *Philippe Duke of Orléans, Regent of France* (1979).

[135] ———, *Liberty and Order in Early Modern Europe. The Subject and the State 1650–1800* (1986).

[136] G. Symcox, *Victor Amadeus II. Absolutism in the Savoyard State 1675–1730* (1983).

[137] C. Tilley (ed.), *The Formation of National States in Western Europe* (1975). Political-science approach.

[138] R. Vierhaus, *Germany in the Age of Absolutism* (1988).

## A militarised society?

[139] T. Barker, *Army, Aristocracy, Monarchy: Essays on War, Society and Government in Austria, 1618–1780* (1982). Densely written, but valuable set of essays.

[140] J. Black (ed.), *The Origins of War in Early Modern Europe* (1987). Wars as products of bellicose elites.

[141] J. Black, *The Rise of the European Powers, 1679–1793* (1990). International relations and their background.

[142] L. and M. Frey, *Societies in Upheaval. Insurrections in France, Hungary, and Spain in the Early Eighteenth Century* (1987).

[143] C. R. Friedrichs, *Urban Society in an Age of War: Nördlingen, 1580–1720* (1979). Effect of war on a German town.

[144] M. P. Gutmann, *War and Rural Life in the Early Modern Low Countries* (1980). Effect of war in Meuse region.

[145] A. J. Hayter, *The Army and the Crowd in mid-Georgian England* (1978).

[146] R. Hellie, *Enserfment and Military Change in Muscovy* (1971).

[147] C. W. Ingrao, *The Hessian Mercenary State. Ideas, Institutions and Reform under Frederick II, 1760–1785* (1987). Excellent study of Hesse-Cassel.

[148] J. L. H. Keep, *Soldiers of the Tsar: Army and Society in Russia, 1462–1872* (1985).

[149] P. Kennedy, *The Rise and Fall of the Great Powers. Economic Change and Military Conflict from 1500 to 2000* (1988). Wide-ranging study that exaggerates role of economic factors and is stronger on post-1815 period.

[150] W. H. McNeill, *The Pursuit of Power: Technology, Armed Force and Society since A.D. 1000* (1982).

[151] J. V. Polisensky (ed.), *War and Society in Europe, 1618–1648* (1978). Valuable on Thirty Years War.

[152] F. Redlich, *The German Military Enterpriser and his Workforce* (1964). Important for mercenaries, recruitment and Thirty Years War.

[153] M. Roberts, *The Age of Liberty. Sweden 1719–1772* (1986).

[154] G. E. Rothenberg, B. K. Kiraly and P. F. Sugar (eds), *East European Society and War in the Pre-Revolutionary Eighteenth Century* (1982).

[155] J. M. Stoye, 'Soldiers and Civilians', *New Cambridge Modern History*, VI (1970). On 1688–1725.

[156] I. A. A. Thompson, *War and Government in Habsburg Spain, 1560–1620* (1976). Scholarly study of administration.

[157] J. R. Western, *The English Militia in the Eighteenth Century. The Story of a Political Issue 1660–1802* (1965). Important account of overlooked institution.

# Index

108